Creative Group Therapy for Women Survivors of Child Sexual Abuse

of related interest

Working with Victims of Crime
Policies, Politics and Practice
Brian Williams
ISBN 1 85302 450 3 pb

Guiding Recovery from Child Sexual Abuse
Horizons of Hope
Dave Simon
ISBN 1 85302 571 2 pb

Good Practice in Counselling People Who Have Been Abused
Edited by Zetta Bear
ISBN 1 85302 424 4 pb

Counselling Adult Survivors of Child Sexual Abuse, 2nd edition
Christiane Sanderson
ISBN 1 85302 252 7 pb

The Essential Groupworker
Teaching and Learning Creative Groupwork
Mark Doel and Catherine Sawdon
ISBN 1 85302 823 1 pb

Grief and Powerlessness
Helping People Regain Control of their Lives
Ruth Bright
ISBN 1 85302 386 8 pb

Contemporary Art Therapy with Adolescents
Shirley Riley
Forewords by Gerald D. Osher and Cathy Malchiodi
ISBN 1 85302 636 0 hb
ISBN 1 85302 637 9 pb

Medical Art Therapy with Adults
Edited by Cathy Malchiodi
Foreword by Judith Rubin
ISBN 1 85302 677 8 pb
ISBN 1 85302 676 X hb

Creative Group Therapy for Women Survivors of Child Sexual Abuse

Speaking the Unspeakable

Bonnie Meekums

Jessica Kingsley Publishers
London and Philadelphia

First published in the United Kingdom in 2000 by
Jessica Kingsley Publishers Ltd
116 Pentonville Road
London N1 9JB, England
and
325 Chestnut Street
Philadelphia, PA 19106, USA

www.jkp.com

Library of Congress Cataloging in Publication Data
Meekums, Bonnie.
Creative group therapy for women survivors of child sexual abuse : speaking the unspeakable / Bonnie Meekums.
p. cm.
Includes bibliographical references (p.) and index.
ISBN 1-85302-543-8 (alk. paper)
1. Adult child sexual abuse victims--Rehabilitation. 2. Group psychotherapy.
3. Art therapy. 4. Dance therapy. 5. Psychodrama. 6. Women--Mental health.
I. Title.
RC569.5.A28 M44 2000
616.85'83690651--dc21   99-056669

British Library Cataloguing in Publication Data
A CIP catalogue record for this book is available from the British Library

ISBN 1 85302 453 8

Printed and Bound in Great Britain by
Athenaeum Press, Gateshead, Tyne and Wear

Contents

Tables

Figures

For George and Violet Meekums

Foreword

During the 1980s and 1990s, our understanding of child sexual abuse has increased dramatically. Much has been written about the prevalence and the effects. We now understand more about how and why it occurs but there is still much work to be done on how we may repair the damage which it causes.

Some of the earlier texts on the subject, for example Sgroi (1982), did offer suggestions for treatment of abused children and adolescents but did not mention specifically adult survivors. It was recognised that many mothers of sexually abused children had also suffered many different kinds of abuse themselves. Any treatment they received, however, was usually in the context of family therapy in which their own history was not addressed. Many women survivors of abuse, who presented at this time to psychiatric services, received medication to control symptoms. In the 1970s and early 1980s women began to reject the 'psychiatric labels' which they felt had been imposed upon them. Women themselves, working together in self-help groups, provided each other with effective support to cope with their own abusive experiences. In the UK, groups like Rape Crisis and Women's Aid assisted women to form such links.

Not surprisingly, there was a mistrust of the professionals involved in working with women, especially those who were working in medical establishments. Recognising the need for skilled help, women turned to social workers and counsellors who were often already working in the community. Sanderson's (1990, 1995) book on counselling adult survivors was a good example of this kind of work. Sanderson acknowledges that she began by helping to set up Incest Survivors Network with other women.

In addition, during the 1980s, many women who were trained as creative arts therapists, or psychodramatists, realised that this kind of work was particularly powerful with those who had suffered sexual abuse. Working within the safety and containment of metaphor, sometimes individually or often in groups, women survivors began to express their feelings, often for the first time. Bonnie Meekums, herself a leading dance movement therapist, working with colleagues trained in dramatherapy and art therapy, began a series of successful groups for women survivors of sexual abuse.

This book is the outcome of this process. It provides a sound academic bedrock of theory based on the author's extensive knowledge of sexual abuse and of her own discipline. In addition she shows her versatility and eclecticism by acknowledging her debt to other arts therapies and psychodrama. I find it impressive to see how she has integrated other therapies in a careful way, without producing a 'ragbag' of techniques. Indeed one of her strengths is the attention she pays to the vital areas of boundaries and safety.

In the second part of the book she stresses the importance of good assessment, something which is often overlooked by inexperienced group practitioners. Her professionalism is also very apparent in this part of the book as she describes very practical ideas for exercises. It is easy to provide suitable 'games' or 'exercises' for use in therapeutic groups but without a good grounding in boundaries and group dynamics they could be counter-productive. There is no danger of that here since the author makes the context of the exercises quite clear.

Dr Meekums is to be congratulated on producing a book which will be warmly welcomed by many professionals working in this difficult but rewarding field of therapy.

References

Sanderson, C. (1990, 1995) *Counselling Adult Survivors of Child Sexual Abuse*, 1st and 2nd edns. London: Jessica Kingsley Publishers.

Sgroi, S. (1982) *Handbook of Clinical Intervention in Child Sexual Abuse*. Lexington, MA: Lexington Books.

Anne Bannister,
Psychodramatist, dramatherapist, playtherapist
October 1999

Acknowledgements

Nothing is ever new. We all build on the wisdom of those who have gone before us. We hope that we remember to acknowledge those trailblazers, inspirers and accomplices in our task. I am deeply aware that, without certain people's help, this book would not have been written. My first debt is to the fourteen women who participated in my doctoral research. Without them, I would have had nothing of value to say. I hope that, in publishing this book, I am doing their words justice and in some small way helping to give new meaning to their suffering and their courage.

I also owe a debt to those people who have struggled with the theory and practice of recovery from child sexual abuse trauma. In particular, I owe a lot to Judith Herman, whose book *Trauma and Recovery* inspired me as I was writing up my own PhD, and validated much of what I had discovered in my own research.

The academic supervision provided by my dear friend and colleague Dr Patricia Sanderson of the University of Manchester was invaluable. She was, as the process required, devil's advocate, text editor, supporter, adviser and advocate. Her contribution went beyond the call of her official role. The clinical supervision I received first from John Casson and then from Anne Bannister was inspirational, and kept me in a healthy position of questioning my own practice. My colleagues, in particular Sue Fletcher, Louise Larkinson, Jacqui Peploe and Paddy Crossling, struggled with me to develop this work and to understand what it was we were trying to do. Sue and Louise both helped to develop the assessment and evaluation materials used in this book.

My employers, Tameside and Glossop Community and Priority Services (NHS) Trust, gave me much valued study time and financial assistance to complete my doctorate. I am particularly grateful to John Archer for his vision in the early days, without which I would never have embarked on the study.

My husband, Philip Spence, entered into our marriage just as I began my research. He has been a tower of strength to me, suffering my long hours at the computer and at times taking more than his fair share of the work that comes with a family. Along with my children Joseph, Rosa and Cameron, he has kept me sane.

Any omissions in the above are simply due to the overwhelming debt of gratitude which I owe to a great number of people. If I have forgotten to name any one individual, it is with the deepest regret.

Finally, I wish to point out that any omissions or inaccuracies in the text are entirely my own responsibility.

Note: Some of the material presented in the theoretical sections of this book has been previously published in *The Arts in Psychotherapy* (1999) *26*, 4, under the title 'A creative model for recovery from child sexual abuse trauma'.

Preface

This book arose out of my own need, as a clinician in the early 1990s, for some guidance on how to work in an adult mental health setting with groups of women who had been sexually victimised as children. Should I be non-directive or provide structure? What techniques and approaches would be useful?

I feared that without guidelines I might do more harm than good, yet there were few guidelines available. At the same time, senior managers were identifying a training need in this area. Ward staff in particular were being flooded by disclosures from patients, responding with different degrees of skill in the absence of formal training.

Thankfully, since that time some excellent books have been written on the subject by experienced clinicians. I have been inspired by Christiane Sanderson's book *Counselling Adult Survivors of Child Sexual Abuse* (1990; now in its second (1995) edition with Jessica Kingsley Publishers), then by Susan Simonds' *Bridging the Silence* (1994) and by Judith Herman's excellent treatise *Trauma and Recovery* (1992). My own work has been an attempt to bridge the research gap by seeking the voices of service users in answer to some of my original questions.

In making use of this book, please do not skip the theoretical chapters in the first part. These provide a logical progression into the practice. The model for recovery from child sexual abuse trauma, which I present in Chapter 3, is essentially an integration of theory and practice. It puts flesh on the bones of the second part, and provides essential detail that should not be missed.

Finally, it is my hope that readers will be able to add their own insights and experience to what is written on these pages. I offer this book, not as the last word on the topic, but as a springboard for further development.

Abbreviations

ADMT(UK)	Association for Dance Movement Therapy UK
BDI	Beck's Depression Inventory
CATs	creative arts therapies
CPSM	Council for the Professions Supplementary to Medicine
CSA	child sexual abuse
DMT	dance movement therapy
FMS	false memory syndrome
GAT-P	group arts therapies programme
ISE	Index of Self-Esteem
IT	interpersonal transaction
LOC	Locus of Control Scale
MCMI	Millon Clinical Multiaxial Inventory
NHS	National Health Service (UK)
RCT	randomised controlled (clinical) trial
SAS	Social Adjustment Scale
SCL-90-R	Symptom Check-List 90 Revised
SSC	Sexual Symptom Checklist
TSC-33	Trauma Symptom Checklist
UKCP	United Kingdom Council for Psychotherapy

PART ONE
Theoretical Concerns

Child Sexual Abuse
An Overview of the Literature

Introduction

In this chapter, I attempt to outline the current state of knowledge about child sexual abuse (CSA). I focus in particular on incidence, that is how prevalent the phenomenon of CSA appears to be; sequelae, that is the commonly reported symptoms and conditions which may potentially be outcomes of CSA; the debate on 'false memory syndrome' (FMS); existing treatment options for those suffering the after-effects of CSA trauma; and previously articulated theories of trauma and recovery.

General incidence of child sexual abuse

While there is considerable literature concerning incidence and sequelae, most of the studies have been retrospective and methodologically flawed, making interpretation difficult (Brière 1992). The extent of CSA as reported in the literature depends largely on the definition used by the researcher and on the research methodology employed. However, when similar methodologies and definitions are employed, there seems to be some agreement, adding some measure of credibility to the findings.

For example, Baker and Duncan (1985) used a similar definition of CSA to that of Finkelhor's (1979) seminal American study of female and male college students. Baker and Duncan's large and representative British study of both men and women revealed a CSA incidence of 13 per cent in the 15–24-year-old age group (age at interview) compared with the 14 per cent reported by Finkelhor. Russell (1983) used a stricter definition of CSA to include only contact experiences in her study of American women. She appears to have gone to even greater lengths than Baker and Duncan (1985) to train interviewers to be sensitive, and arrived at the conclusion that 12 per cent had been sexually abused within the family before the age of 14. This is interesting, since it corresponds to Baker and Duncan's overall figure of 12 per cent of the girls in her sample having suffered some form of CSA, although the incidence of intrafamilial sexual abuse prior to the age of 18 years reported by Russell was 16 per cent.

Russell (1983) found that 20 per cent of those interviewed reported extrafamilial abuse before the age of 14 years, which is higher than Baker and Duncan's (1985) figures. This difference may be due to interviewing techniques; it is possible that Baker and Duncan's 12 per cent were largely abused by familiar adults, whereas Russell was specifically focusing on the differences between intrafamilial and extrafamilial abuse and using a definition which did not exclude young people as perpetrators. Russell may therefore have been more likely to discover incidences in the respondent's childhood which, while experienced as abusive to young girls, are perhaps accepted as the norm and perpetrated by peers. Russell (1983) found that almost half of the respondents reported some form of unwanted sexual experience before the age of 14 years when including both contact and non-contact, intrafamilial and extrafamilial definitions.

Retrospective studies such as these are likely to result in underestimates of the incidence of CSA, since some respondents would probably wish to avoid reliving painful memories by admitting to the history of CSA (Baker and Duncan 1985). However, so far as the research indicates at present, we can identify the following probabilities:

- Social class does not affect the likelihood of CSA (Baker and Duncan 1985).

- For actual physical contacts between adults and children of a sexual nature, between one in six and one in four girls are victims (Nash and West 1985), whereas the figure is nearer to one in two when one includes other unwanted sexual contacts, including those perpetrated by peers (Russell 1983).

- Girls are more likely to be sexually abused than boys, by a factor of between 3:2 and 2:1 (Baker and Duncan 1985; Wellman 1993), although both sexes are approached in equal numbers by potential abusers (Wellman 1993).

- Female victims tend to be more likely to be abused before the age of 10, by a close family member, whereas male victims tend to be older and abused by someone outside the family but known to them (Baker and Duncan 1985).

- Girls are slightly more likely than boys to be abused by a complete stranger (Baker and Duncan 1985).

- Overall, at least half of all abusers are known to their victims (Baker and Duncan 1985; Russell 1983).

- Where only single incidents of abuse are reported, the perpetrator is significantly more likely to be a stranger to the victim. Conversely, repeated abuse by the same perpetrator tends to be associated with familiar adults (Baker and Duncan 1985).

- Most abusers are male; only 4 per cent of perpetrators were stated as female in Russell's (1983) study. This figure may be an underestimate, since it is only since the 1980s that abuse by females has become the topic of both professional and media discussion.

- Of very serious child sexual abuse (rape or oral sex), 74 per cent of perpetrators are known to the child (Mrazek, Lynch and Bentovim 1983) and very few are women (Russell 1983, 1984). Of the abuse perpetrated by stepfathers, 47 per cent falls into this category (Russell 1983, 1984).

- The overall incidence of very serious abuse coming to the attention of British general practitioners, police surgeons, paediatricians and child psychiatrists is three per thousand of the population, most of these being girls (Mrazek et al. 1983).

- Only 2 per cent of cases of intrafamilial abuse are ever reported to any authority (Russell 1983).

In other words, previously trusted male adults tend to abuse more often (though not necessarily more children) than strangers, although only 14 per cent of abusers are family members. Most of this intrafamilial abuse never comes to the attention of the authorities, and the most serious forms of CSA are perpetrated within this group, including that by stepfathers. The rest of the half known to victims are presumably made up of (predominantly male) teachers, priests, babysitters and the like; in other words, people who have access to children through other means than family ties.

Wellman's (1993) finding that, while boys are less often sexually abused than girls they are approached in equal numbers, is an interesting one. She examined the attitudes, beliefs and recall of 824 American college students concerning CSA, and found that the women expressed stronger pro-social beliefs and attitudes, and stronger emotional reactions to abuse than the men. She concludes that the differential between approach and completed act of abuse is due to the different socialisation of males and females:

> Historically in America, we have socialized females differently from males. Through the processes of conditioning and social learning, males have learned to be competent, self-sufficient and non-disclosing, while females have been socialized to be warm, nurturant and expressive (Wellman 1993, p.545).

It could be argued that this observation holds true not just in the United States but also in the United Kingdom and in other countries with similar social structures. CSA was defined by Wellman (1993) as unwanted sexual contact during childhood or adolescence. There was no significant difference between women and men regarding the identity of the abuser, a fact which may be skewed by the non-representative sample, but which does potentially lend some support to Wellman's (1993) interpretation of her findings.

Bagley (1990) suggests that the prevalence of CSA may be decreasing, due to greater information via the media and raised awareness among both the general public and professionals who may act to stop or prevent it. This, he argues, mitigates against negative trends such as the growing incidence of stepfathers in families. His survey of 750 women aged 18 to 27 years revealed greater reporting of CSA with increase in age of the respondent from 18 (20.8 per cent) to 21 years (33.3 per cent), followed by a reduction at age 22 years (24 per cent) and then an increase up to 24 years of age (42 per cent), after which the incidence again dropped and remained static (around 35 per cent). Bagley looked at media exposure: about half (52.1 per cent) of 18- and 19-year-olds had experienced media presentations concerning child sexual abuse, compared with only 17.6 per cent of 20 to 27-year-olds. Two-thirds of all media presentations reported by the respondents had occurred during their school years. However, it could be argued that this may not be entirely responsible for the lower reporting of CSA in the younger age group. Perhaps more significant is the fact that the incidence of reported CSA increased steadily during the years associated with either college or immersion into the world of work. It may be that this exposure to the more adult world increases the young adult's awareness of the issues. Similarly, the greater reporting in the age group of 24 years may be due to life events, for example a committed relationship or even parenthood forcing again greater awareness. The incidence thereafter is not dissimilar to that at age 21. Bagley (1990) suggests that since the older subjects were more likely to have been abused for the first time during adolescence (age 14 plus) than younger subjects, the increased publicity surrounding CSA may be protecting the younger age group. This may be a serious flaw in logic. It may be that that the younger subjects were more protected from one form of CSA, namely that perpetrated by peers on adolescent girls. Increased awareness of the right to say no may mean that more young women are asserting their right to choose when, how and with whom they experiment sexually. However, the abuse of young girls, as I have outlined, is often perpetrated by trusted adults, serious in nature, and undisclosed. Awareness of the right to say no may not have reached these very young victims, and may be ineffective in the face of a powerful adult.

The general conclusion of incidence studies is that CSA is by no means a rare occurrence; this is an important conclusion, in light of the 'false memory syndrome' (FMS) debate (see pp.28–30). CSA is not a problem which is going to disappear overnight. It is also an international problem (Finkelhor 1994). More relevant to this book, however, is the incidence of a history of CSA in psychotherapy and psychiatry populations.

Incidence of child sexual abuse in psychiatry and psychotherapy

Psychiatric patients are more likely to report CSA as defined by Finkelhor (1979), than general practice attenders, in a ratio of 3:2 (Palmer *et al.* 1993), which may be compatible with a causal role. My re-examination of Palmer *et al.*'s data (Meekums 1998) shows that the negative mental health effects of intercourse before the age of 13 years were greater than those of intercourse occurring from 13 to 15 years. Full intercourse under the age of 13 was reported more than seven times more in the psychiatric group than in the control. This observation may be partly explicable in terms of the possibility that during the teenage years some intercourse occurs between boyfriend and girlfriend and is less traumatic, especially since Finkelhor's overall definition of CSA does not imply that the sexual contact was necessarily unwanted. Palmer *et al.*'s (1993) own interview data would seem to lend some support to my argument.

Sheldon (1988) studied documentation relating to 115 women who had been referred to a regional psychotherapy unit in the UK. She found that 19 (16.5 per cent) of these women were identified at the time of referral as having suffered CSA and a further 5 (4.3 per cent) made covert references. The percentage making overt references is again similar to Russell's (1983) figures for intrafamilial abuse. Sheldon (1988) used a definition of CSA which may have particularly highlighted the incidence of incest, in that she used criteria of age and familiarity. She found a higher incidence of psychiatric morbidity in the group which was not identified with CSA, a fact which on the face of it is confusing if one accepts the viewpoint that CSA is potentially damaging to mental health. However, Sheldon argues that the abused group was younger and therefore less likely to have developed a mental health label. Moreover, the group not identified as having been abused might in fact have been abused but be less able to disclose this, potentially contributing to their mental health difficulties. Unfortunately, this last point is not supported by Sheldon with any research evidence to suggest that disclosure *per se* is beneficial to mental health. Notwithstanding this shortcoming in her argument, many clinicians would agree that disclosure of what the client views as the 'relevant account' is an important part of therapy (see e.g. Jones 1991). Herman (1992) has presented some research evidence for the claim that narration of the account has therapeutic value.

The controversy surrounding the possible existence of FMS (Morton *et al.* 1995) makes the figures for the incidence of CSA in mental health and psychotherapy settings more difficult to interpret. However, in a small audit of the psychotherapy services at one British hospital, approximately half of the 81 cases according to their therapists had reported some form of child abuse, most of these having suffered more than one type (Meekums 1996). A high proportion of these presented with a risk of self-harming, and similarly high proportions had diagnosed depression and/or anxiety-related symptoms. This is a much higher incidence of CSA than those reported above, but is remarkably close to Craine *et al.*'s (1988) figure of 51 per cent. My own audit included cases of long-standing, allowing for more disclosure after the referral stage (Meekums 1996). Craine *et al.* (1988) used a sample of 105 female patients from nine state hospitals. Each volunteer was administered a structured interview, which had been designed to elicit a history of sexual victimisation. Over half (56 per cent) of those with a history of CSA had never been identified as such during the course of their treatment. Further support for Craine *et al.*'s (1988) and my own (Meekums 1996) figures is to be found in a small study by Walker and James (1992). In Walker and James' sample of 51 psychiatric patients, 49 per cent gave a history of CSA, 48 per cent a history of physical abuse, and 30 per cent a history of both. Only 28 per cent of those found to have a history of CSA had disclosed this at their initial clinical interview.

Given the clinical evidence that clients find it difficult to disclose a history of CSA, the prevalence estimates by Meekums (1996), Craine *et al.* (1988) and Walker and James (1992) in psychiatric populations are probably more reliable than that of Sheldon (1988). They may still be an underestimate of the extent of the problem.

The higher incidence of CSA in the psychiatric population than in the general population provides some evidence for a causal link between CSA and certain kinds of mental health outcomes. Nevertheless, caution must be exercised in assumptions about outcome; by no means all CSA victims will go on to develop mental health problems. Emotional abuse appears to be a stronger predictor of poor mental health outcome than CSA alone, but where histories of both emotional abuse and CSA are present, the effect is more than doubled. When physical abuse is also present in the history, the negative effects on mental health are potentially even greater (Bagley 1995).

Sequelae

Long-term effects of CSA are difficult to elicit. The literature is considerable, although as with incidence studies methodologies and definitions vary, making comparisons difficult. There is a need for more longitudinal and controlled studies (Brière 1992). There are several reviews of the literature concerning alleged outcomes of CSA (Beitchman *et al.* 1992; Browne and Finkelhor 1986; Cahill, Llewelyn and Pearson 1991; Green 1993; Sheldrick 1991) and Jumper (1995) has carried out a meta-analysis of the reports relating to CSA and adult psychological adjustment. Jumper's (1995) analysis indicates a statistically significant risk of depression, low self-esteem, and other psychological symptomatology, most marked in community or clinical samples rather than college samples. She also notes the need for more studies that differentiate the effects of CSA from other traumata.

An examination of primary sources shows that the range of long-term effects suggested by research studies includes the following:

- psychosexual dysfunction and relationship problems (Craine *et al.* 1988; Dent-Brown 1993; Fromuth 1986; Herman, Russell and Trocki 1986; Hulme and Grove 1994; Mullen *et al.* 1994; Tsai, Feldman-Summers and Edgar 1979)

- depression (Bagley and Ramsey 1986; Bagley, Wood and Young 1994; Brière and Runtz 1988; Hulme and Grove 1994; Sedney and Brooks 1984)
- anxiety (Brière and Runtz 1988; Sedney and Brooks 1984)
- self-harm and suicide attempts (Bagley and Ramsey 1986; Bagley et al 1994; Brown and Anderson 1991; Dent-Brown 1993; Sedney and Brooks 1984)
- psychosis (Bagley and Ramsey 1986)
- revictimisation, which includes adult rape and the tendency to form relationships with abusive partners (Dent-Brown 1993; Miller et al. 1978)
- chronic pelvic pain or other somatisation (Brière and Runtz 1988; Gross et al. 1980; Morrison 1989; Walker et al. 1988)
- diagnostic categories of borderline or hysterical personality traits and other personality disorders (Brown and Anderson 1991; Gross et al. 1980; McClelland et al. 1991)
- dissociation, which includes the sense of 'not being in one's body' (Brière and Runtz 1988; Chu and Dill 1990)
- eating disorders (McClelland et al. 1991)
- drug and alcohol misuse (Brown and Anderson 1991; Craine et al. 1988)
- epilepsy (Greig and Betts 1992)
- bowel disease (Walker et al. 1993).

Symptomatology is generally more developed in women whose abuse was perpetrated by a father-figure, where there was genital contact, or where force was used (Browne and Finkelhor 1986; Herman et al. 1986; Sedney and Brooks 1984).

Bagley (1995) suggests that the mental health consequences for those with a history of emotional, physical and sexual abuse are likely to be more negative than for those who have suffered sexual abuse alone. His data relate to a Canadian community mental health survey of 735 women aged 18 to 27, all of whom agreed to be interviewed in their own home. CSA was defined as an unwanted sexual contact prior to the age of 16. Emotional and physical abuse were measured using a valid and reliable scale, the 'memories of childhood rearing scale' (Perris et al. 1980). Various measures of adult adjustment were used, including the Trauma Symptom Checklist (TSC-33) (Brière and Runtz 1989), a valid and reliable scale.

Bagley (1995) found that 32 per cent of women had experienced at least one episode of CSA, which is rather higher than some of the studies quoted above. Furthermore 16.9 per cent of the sample had experienced what Bagley (1995) defines as a more serious form of CSA, that is either repeated sexual abuse, involving contact; or with penetration; or perpetrated by a father figure. Following a cluster analysis, Bagley found that CSA only atypically occurs alone; that is, it is usually accompanied by some other form of abuse.

In Bagley's (1995) study, 68 per cent of those with a history of both emotional and sexual abuse had high scores on the TSC-33 (Brière and Runtz 1989), an effect which is higher than the additive effects of emotional abuse alone (24 per cent) plus sexual abuse alone (11 per cent). Bagley found that 85 per cent of those with a history of physical, emotional and sexual abuse had high scores. Emotional abuse, not sexual abuse, was the strongest predictor of negative mental health consequences. However, as Bagley (1995) points out, CSA remains morally wrong. His justification for this statement is that there is no certainty that a child will not suffer in the short or long term. My own standpoint is that CSA is wrong because it is an abuse of power.

One possible explanation for the phenomenon discovered by Bagley's (1995) research might be that those who have support at the time of the abuse, for example from a believing and protective mother-figure, are less likely to be damaged by the experience than those whose experience is denied. For example, if the family is supportive and neither parent is physically or emotionally abusive, it is more likely that in the event of sexual abuse by a stranger the mother-figure will respond in a protective way. However, if she is failing to protect already from emotional or physical abuse (for whatever reason), or is herself abusive in these ways, she is less likely to be able to protect the child from sexual abuse. Bagley (1995) found that girls who experienced all three forms of abuse were least likely to disclose this, whereas those that experienced CSA alone were most likely to inform others. Those least likely to be believed or most likely to be blamed were girls who suffered both sexual and physical abuse, and not being believed, or being blamed, was a powerful predictor of negative mental health outcome.

Bagley's (1995) study was probably in publication when Mullen *et al.* (1994) published their own results of a survey of 2250 British women, followed by interviews with 248 CSA victims and an equal number of controls. While focusing exclusively on social, interpersonal and sexual function, they noted that CSA was more common in families which were disturbed or disrupted and in those where emotional and physical abuse was also reported. The significant association between CSA and negative outcome in terms of social, interpersonal and sexual functioning was explicable in part, though not completely, by these associations.

A much earlier study by Fromuth (1986) of 386 American female college students showed that when parental support was controlled for, many of the apparently negative effects of CSA became insignificant, with the exception of sexual revictimisation and phobic anxiety. CSA victims were also more likely to describe themselves as promiscuous, although this seems to have been due to damage of their self-concept, as their behaviour did not differ significantly from the control group. Fromuth's study incorporated only a healthy sample, and so she may have missed those harmed most by their experience. The definition of CSA used was also wide-ranging, including experiences that may have been less harmful. Bagley (1995) acknowledges that his study was carried out prior to the publication of Alexander's (1992) treatise on attachment theory and sexual abuse, although he refers to her work in his discussion. Alexander's hypothesis remains untested empirically, although she presents some powerful arguments both from a theoretical perspective and in citing the empirical studies of researchers in the field of attachment theory. Her theory is briefly discussed in the section on trauma-genics (pp.30–34).

A few writers claim positive sequelae, for example McMillen et al. (1995), who defined CSA as unwanted sexual contact before the age of 14. They used interviews and questionnaires with 154 low-income women who had been sexually abused as children. Almost half of the volunteers reported some benefit. Perceived benefits fell into four main categories: protecting children from abuse; self-protection; increased knowledge of CSA; and having a stronger personality. However, 88.9 per cent of those perceiving benefit also perceived harm. Herman et al. (1986), comparing a community sample of 152 women with a clinical sample of 53 women, found that about half of the community sample said that they had recovered well from their abuse. The effects of social stigmatisation on mental health service users should not be ignored when considering the validity of the results of both Herman et al.'s (1986) and McMillen et al.'s (1995) studies: to admit to not having recovered might be interpreted as a sign of mental health 'weakness'.

Herman (1992) suggests, following a detailed review of the literature concerning trauma, that many of the symptoms experienced by adult survivors of CSA are sequelae associated with any chronic trauma perpetrated by human acts. She cites the experience of Holocaust victims, war veterans from Vietnam and political hostages to illustrate her case, and proposes the new diagnostic category of 'complex post-traumatic stress disorder'. She also examines in particular the experiences of children who are abused. One fundamental difference, claims Herman, is that: 'Repeated trauma in adult life erodes the structure of the personality already formed, but repeated trauma in childhood forms and deforms the personality' (Herman 1992, p.96).

Herman (1992) writes of the 'omnipresent fear of death' (p.98) experienced by the abused child. The act of silencing is often reinforced by threats of harm to the child or to those she loves, and there is an 'overwhelming sense of helplessness' (p.98). Many of these children, Herman writes (and my own clinical experience would seem to bear witness to Herman's claim), experience torture and imprisonment akin to that experienced by political imprisonment. The child responds, as Herman and others have observed, by trying to hide, by trying to appease, and by developing a hypervigilance often described as 'frozen watchfulness'. The child's perception of abandonment by the non-abusive parent is often viewed as a greater betrayal than that by the abuser.

One crucial development for the child is that, in realising she is unable to alter reality, she alters instead the way she views and experiences it. It is this need to cope with the experience of abuse which, Herman (1992) and others have claimed, leads the child to blame herself for what is happening. This is preferable to believing that the trusted adult is bad: 'it enables her to preserve a sense of meaning, hope, and power. If she is bad, then her parents are good. If she is bad, then she can try to be good' (Herman 1992, p.103).

This perception may be reinforced, Herman reminds the reader, by parental scapegoating. The survivor also learns to pretend that the abuse is not happening, through numbing or possibly even out-of-body experiences.

Herman (1992) interprets the self-cutting practised by some survivors of childhood abuse as an attempt to deal with emotional pain. Far from being associated with suicide attempts or with cries for help (although both of these may also occur) it is an act of self-preservation, often carried out in secret.

False memory syndrome

Since the early 1990s, there has been much talk of FMS. This alleged condition is the result, it is argued, of poor therapists applying dangerous therapy techniques to innocent victims, and thus implanting false memories of abuse. The movement appears to have arisen from litigation in the USA and later in the UK, with those accused claiming to have had their lives ruined by allegations of abuse perpetrated by them on their daughters. Some daughters have since retracted their accusations, lending weight to the arguments of campaign groups like the British False Memory Society. The movement has stimulated much debate and also research. The popular press has shown interest in the issue (for example, Grant 1994; Morton 1994; Waterhouse and Strickland 1994), and whole conferences, including 'Memories of Abuse' held in 1995 in Sheffield, have been devoted to the topic.

A discussion of FMS is important in considering the potentially powerful, but contentious aspects of any treatment option that facilitates recall. It could be argued that the kind of therapy proposed in this book falls into this category. The model for recovery developed through my research (Meekums 1998) and discussed in Chapter 3 of this book demonstrates a role for the creative arts therapies in raising to consciousness various aspects of the individual's past. Memories thus become more real in the present so that they can be confronted and expressed in the safety of the therapeutic milieu and in the presence of benevolent witnesses. The model suggests that, following this process, new perspectives can be adopted. It should be noted here that at no time did the therapists who contributed to my research attempt to make suggestions as to the nature of memories emerging. The issue of verification for legal purposes was not present; of central importance was the survivor's own interpretation of her experience. Kane's (1989) distinction may be helpful, between, on the one hand, what she calls 'fantastica', which are 'a mere conceit, something ridiculous and insubstantial' (p.25), lacking the balance of sensation and the mediation of thinking and feeling functions, and on the other hand, true imagination, which is 'the real, literal power of the soul to create images' (p.25). The model proposed in Chapter 3, and the therapy on which my research was based, both emphasise the use of what Kane calls 'true imagination', in relation to actual memories.

There is evidence from psychological research that it is possible to implant memories (Fonagy and Target 1995), suggesting that false memories can be created about CSA. However, their existence may not be as prevalent as claimed by the British False Memory Society. The evidence against the prevalence of false memories lies in several facts. These include that recovered memories of abuse rarely arise from total amnesia (Morton *et al.* 1995); the clarity and detail in early personal accounts (for example Angelou 1984; Spring 1987), which preceded any media 'hype' about the issue and some of which have been written by well-respected academics and writers (including Angelou 1984); the fact that survivors of severe abuse may suffer from self-doubt concerning the truth of their own memories (Cahill *et al.* 1991) and often do have impaired memory function (Fonagy and Target 1995); and in the systematic silencing of abuse victims discussed by Masson (1992) and dating back to Freud (1896) and beyond. Olafson, Corwin and Summit (1993) argue that in modern history the social awareness of CSA has endured cycles of discovery and suppression, and that the current backlash has many of the hallmarks of that which followed Freud's (1896) link between hysteria and CSA. Herman (1992) also describes in some detail the history of what she describes as 'episodic amnesia' (p.7) regarding the study of psychological trauma. This, she observes, dates from the early studies of hysteria in the nineteenth century, through studies of 'shell-shocked' soldiers during the First World War and later studies of Vietnam veterans, to the present concern of CSA trauma. The contemporary academic and public interest in CSA arose directly out of the consciousness-raising groups of the women's movement in the late 1960s and early 1970s.

Williams (1994) provides powerful evidence for the probability that many abuse victims never recall the event on any conscious level. In a study of 129 women with histories of CSA which had been recorded by the authorities when those women were children, she found that on interview 38 per cent did not recall the events of 17 years earlier. The probability of amnesia was increased by the identity of the perpetrator being someone the victim knew and by the victim being under 7 years of age at the time of the offence. Williams (1994) concludes that the absence of memory should not be taken as evidence that abuse did not occur. She does not appear to consider the possibility that the professionals who had recorded the incidence of CSA at the time might have been wrong. The experience of the much-publicised Cleveland and Orkney cases in Britain brought into question the validity of claims made by social workers and others concerning the existence of CSA in those cases. Nevertheless, it could be argued that it is unlikely that properly trained professionals would be incorrect in the majority of cases recorded, and it should be remembered that Russell (1983) found that only 2 per cent of intrafamilial abuse is ever reported.

Loftus (1994) cautions against the use of extensive 'memory work', a category of therapy into which she places 'regression, body memory interpretation, suggestive questioning, guided visualisation, sexualised dream interpretation, aggressive sodium amytal interviews, misleading bibliotherapy, or any of a number of other suspect techniques' (p.443). The inclusion of guided visualisation in this list calls into question much of the therapy practised by arts therapists (for example, Levens 1994), and on the face of it does not sit obviously alongside the rest of Loftus' (1994) list. Some kinds of guided visualisation, like that of Levens (1994), leave the client to fill in the important gaps, while others (not practised by any creative arts therapist whose clinical work I have ever known) might be suggestive of actual events. It may be that Loftus was referring to the latter.

It is also unclear what Loftus (1994) means by 'body memory interpretation'. Some highly respected cognitive behavioural therapists are becoming interested in the notion of 'body memory' (Hackman 1999), as mediated through the 'felt sense' (a term presumably borrowed from Gendlin 1981). Hackman (1999) describes making use of this 'felt sense' to access traumatic memories prior to re-attribution of their meaning through reworking the memories. The manner of reworking described by Hackman is similar to that described in Chapter 6 of this book (see, for example, the sections on myths and stories, drawing the cause, and letters). In any event, Loftus (1994) makes the useful suggestion that group therapy should not be offered until clients are sure that their memories are real.

Notwithstanding the potential occurrence of false memories, it is crucial in order to repair the damage of the past that therapists believe the clients when they present with actual memories. This is not to say that therapists should believe everyone who claims to be a survivor simply because of a given set of mental health symptoms and in the absence of actual memories. Clearly, much damage can be done in interpreting a set of symptoms as necessarily arising from the experience of abuse, as for example proposed by Blume (1990).

Traumagenics

From the research cited above concerning the range of sequelae to CSA, it is likely that there is no one theory that can fully explain the trauma experienced by some survivors of CSA. However, an understanding of traumagenics is important in both explaining sequelae and in appreciating the starting point for recovery.

Alexander (1992) presents a conceptual framework for understanding the aetiology of CSA trauma within attachment theory. She cites the evidence for poor attachments playing an aetiological role in CSA traumagenics by reference to previous research. This includes the fact that attachment theory has for some time been used to explain the existence of physical abuse. Also, certain family characteristics are associated with an increased risk of CSA, for example maternal unavailability or the presence of a stepfather. Moreover, long-term effects of CSA are associated with family variables including the support of the non-abused parent. Finally, memories of abuse are often triggered around crises of attachment, including the birth of the first child or the development of a significant relationship. Space does not allow here for a full breakdown of Alexander's hypothesis, which addresses each type of insecure attachment (avoidant, resistant, disorganised) in relation to commonly reported symptomatology. Alexander recommends longitudinal studies to test her hypothesis, though none have been completed to date so far as I am aware.

An earlier, and still generally accepted attempt to create a theory which might explain the traumatic impact of CSA, was developed by Finkelhor and Browne (1985). They identify four traumagenic dynamics: traumatic sexualisation, betrayal, stigmatisation and powerlessness. They argue that different experiences of CSA contain different degrees of trauma in each of these areas, which will predispose the victim to different sequelae. Finkelhor and Browne's model does not appear to be in conflict with that of Alexander (1992). For example, they point out that the traumagenic dynamics must take into account the before- and after-abuse scenarios. A child who is relatively unstigmatised by the abuse may be more stigmatised by the reactions of others to her disclosure. Another child may already be so disempowered or feel so betrayed by her family dynamics including possible physical and/or emotional abuse that sexual abuse compounds these effects. Finkelhor and Browne (1985) suggest that an understanding of these dynamics can aid assessment and thus influence the type of intervention offered to a client. For example, they suggest that where stigmatisation is likely to have occurred a group therapeutic approach might be beneficial. I would suggest that in this society, we have a long way to go before victims of sexual abuse are free from stigmatisation. A group therapy approach at some stage in the recovery process may therefore be indicated for most people recovering from CSA trauma. The specific dynamics present may also predict the course of recovery, it could be argued; my own clinical experience seems to suggest that the most pervasive or earliest dynamic may be the last to be resolved.

Herman (1992) provides a more recent analysis of trauma and recovery. Through a scholarly review of the literature concerning post-traumatic states, she draws an analogy between the combat neurosis suffered by soldiers during the First World War and the Vietnam war, for example, and the experiences of women in what she describes as 'the sex war' (p.28). Herman claims that 'violence is a routine part of women's sexual and domestic lives' (p.28). She points out that, when the diagnosis of post-traumatic stress disorder was first incorporated into the American Psychiatric Association's manual in 1980, the definition of traumatic events as 'outside the range of usual human experience' (p.33) was already inaccurate. She defends the claim thus: 'Rape, battery, and other forms of sexual and domestic violence are so common a part of women's lives that they can hardly be described as outside the range of ordinary experience' (Herman 1992, p.33).

Herman's (1992) own suggestion is that what makes traumatic events extraordinary is not that they are rare but that they 'overwhelm the ordinary adaptations to life' (p.33). She analyses the common symptoms of post-traumatic states in terms of three categories:

- *hyperarousal*, which includes nightmares, psychosomatic complaints, startle responses, difficulties in sleeping and irritability or aggression

- *intrusion*, which refers primarily to the intrusion of memories that may be encoded either somatically, iconically, or behaviourally via compulsive re-enactments of traumatic situations in an attempt to gain some mastery of the situation

- *constriction or numbing*, similar to a trance state, which may involve suppression or fragmentation of memories and a diminished sense of a future, and may involve also the use of alcohol or narcotics.

Herman (1992) postulates that the opposing states of intrusion and constriction represent an attempt by the individual to find a balance, but that neither actually assists integration of and thus recovery from the traumatic event. She suggests that, following the trauma, intrusion is likely to dominate but that constriction is likely to follow.

Herman's (1992) thesis goes a long way towards setting CSA and other child abuse trauma in a context which might be more easily understood by those for whom the subject is removed from their own experience. By drawing analogies with combat neurosis, she places the experience of women and children within the realm of experience which can also be understood by men who may or may not have been abused as children, and she gives the phenomenon a heroic context. However, Herman does not stop there: she acknowledges that the diagnosis of post-traumatic stress disorder does not adequately account for the complex symptom picture often seen in adult psychiatry. In attempting to explain this complex symptom picture, Herman draws on the research relating to Holocaust survivors and others suffering repeated trauma inflicted during captivity. She notes that many survivors of childhood abuse acquire the diagnostic labels of either somatisation disorder, borderline personality disorder or multiple personality disorder. Of these, the diagnosis of borderline personality disorder, she suggests, is the most pejorative. My own clinical experience suggests that the diagnosis of borderline personality disorder appears to be more frequently used in the UK than that of multiple personality disorder, which in turn is more frequently referred to in the American literature. Herman's new diagnostic category of 'complex post-traumatic stress disorder' encompasses all three of these personality disorder diagnoses and the old category (no longer used) of hysteria, while acknowledging the particular history and sequelae associated with chronic traumata.

One possible criticism of Herman's (1992) thesis is that, while the feminist analysis of a 'sex war' may explain trauma arising from rape and domestic violence, it does not wholly explain trauma resulting from CSA. The latter can be perpetrated by women as well as men (although so far as we know women do not offend in the same numbers as men). In order to explain this phenomenon, one needs to use a more general analysis of power relationships. While Herman does implicitly acknowledge the possibility that women may become perpetrators, she does not go so far as to extend her analysis to include this. Neither does she appear to question the fact that the only war trauma which appears to have been studied in depth is that of the fighting men, rather than for example the women and children who lived in cities which were heavily bombed during the Second World War. Anecdotally, these experiences appear also to have been traumatic, but may have been of less interest to the academics of the time.

One important difference between the trauma of combat neurosis and that of CSA is that the child usually feels totally isolated from any sense of comradeship. While for men in combat one of the most horrifying events is to witness a comrade's death, for the child alone in a darkened room with a loved and previously trusted adult the abuse happens to her, and her alone. Secrecy, betrayal, isolation and stigmatisation, claims Herman (1992), are typical features of chronic child abuse. While Herman also indicates that the combat neurosis is more severe in soldiers for whom these features exist, they are by no means universal experiences associated with wartime combat. If one interrogates the comparison in the light of Finkelhor and Browne's (1985) traumagenics, only powerlessness remains as a potentially common factor in the two kinds of experience.

Existing treatment options

General overview of treatment options

Treatments models for survivors of CSA who present with mental health needs vary to the same extent as treatments for any other psychological problem. These include cognitive therapy (Jehu, Gazan and Klassen 1988), a combination of relaxation and visual-kinaesthetic dissociation (A. Hossack, personal communication 1996; Hossack and Bentall 1996), group therapy (e.g. Alexander et al. 1989; Darongkamas et al. 1995), systemic therapy (Jones 1991), counselling (Sanderson 1990, 1995), psychodrama (Bannister 1991; Karp 1991) and the creative arts therapies (Hagood 1992; Pendzik 1988; Rogers 1994; Serrano 1989; Simonds 1992; Volkman 1993). There are also some references in the literature to more minor therapies, for example voice therapy (Bagley and Young 1990), some which describe integrated specialist projects (Smith et al. 1995), and some accounts that describe the specific context of adult mental health (for example, den Herder and Redner 1991). Den Herder and Redner (1991) identified decreases in medication and in self-harming rates among those who completed sixty sessions of group therapy, which might indicate a useful way of evaluating future interventions.

A small amount of research has been done to evaluate outcomes in therapy for CSA survivors although Cahill et al. (1991) and Dempster and Roberts (1991) point out that very little of the literature is experimentally based. Since randomised controlled clinical trials (RCTs) are generally accepted as the best way to establish causal links, it is important to be cautious in interpreting research. However, it should also be remembered that large sample sizes, and effective control groups which are matched for all the major variables, are often difficult to obtain when testing an innovation.

Dempster and Roberts (1991) attempted to apply the experimental method to the study of a therapeutic programme for sexually abused children, following Finkelhor's (1986) advice that they could be compared with a non-abused group in treatment. They do not define the nature of the therapeutic programme on offer other than to state that this was provided by a specialist team in the Department of Child Psychiatry. The research was thwarted by the fact that Dempster and Roberts (1991) found that the control group of eighteen children contained two who disclosed CSA during treatment, and for a further six children CSA was strongly suspected.

Berry (1997) provides a useful summary of the research concerning CSA, in which she also reviews the evidence for which treatment approach might be most helpful. It should be noted here that Berry is referring to therapy options for CSA survivors as a whole, and not necessarily to the relatively small percentage who go on to develop mental health problems severe enough to indicate referral to a mental health service. Nevertheless, her conclusions warrant some discussion here. Berry appears to argue for an approach based on techniques which concern themselves primarily with here-and-now issues. This may be the preferred treatment option for those whose traumatisation is not sufficiently severe to warrant referral to the mental health services, or for those who would be severely retraumatised by work that focused directly on memories. My own clinical experience, however, reflected also in the work of Herman (1992), is that there is a group of clients for whom some specific work on memories is demanded, and for whom this appears to be an important step in recovery.

Gelinas (1983) argues that unless the underlying trauma of CSA is addressed, clients who present for treatment with what she describes as the 'disguised presentation' of the incest victim will become repetitive treatment seekers. For her part, Alexander (1992) claims that any therapy which fails to address the attachment issues surrounding the abuse will neither aid recovery nor protect against future abuse.

There has been no systematic study to my knowledge that compares, for example, cognitive-behavioural approaches and creative arts therapy approaches in a controlled study. It would be important in any such study that scores in a range of tests to elicit both levels of symptomatology and degree of trauma were similar pre-treatment. Parry and Richardson (1996) argue that, while cognitive-behavioural therapy is the most researched of the psychotherapies, being the most amenable to the experimental method, it should not be assumed that other psychotherapeutic approaches are invalid. They add a caution, that when a particular approach is shown to be harmful this finding should be taken seriously.

Berry (1997) also reviews the qualities of the therapist which seem to best aid recovery. Broadly, these fit with what is known about psychotherapy in general in that the therapeutic alliance is a key factor, including therapist qualities of empathy, warmth and genuineness (Rogers 1957). It should also be remembered that the factors affecting outcome in psychotherapy are much more complex than at one time suspected. They include client-related factors, for example levels and types of symptomatology (Mitchell, Bozarth and Krauft 1977) and motivation (Luborsky *et al.* 1988), and the therapist's adherence to a clear, workable therapeutic approach (Luborsky *et al.* 1988).

Research studies in group therapy for CSA survivors

There have been a few research studies of group treatment programmes for CSA survivors. One early attempt to compare two group treatments was made by Alexander *et al.* (1989). They recruited sixty-five women via the media, to participate in ten-week groups for women who had been abused by fathers, stepfathers or other male relatives. There was no concurrent individual therapy, although serious suicidal ideation was an exclusion criterion, as was substance misuse or psychosis. Despite this care, seven of the women did not complete the programme; three of these became suicidal during their treatment and requested hospitalisation. A range of measures was used to indicate mental state, including Beck's Depression Inventory (BDI) (Beck 1978), the Social Adjustment Scale (SAS) (Weissman and Paykel 1974) and the Symptom Check-List 90 Revised (SCL-90-R) (Derogatis 1983). All of these measures had been shown to have validity for the study. All subjects completed these measures, then were randomly assigned either to a waiting list control, an interpersonal transaction (IT) group, or a group process group. Those in the waiting list control group were retested twelve weeks later, while the two 'experimental' groups were retested following therapy and at six-month follow-up. There were eight therapy groups in all, four in each format. All were conducted by doctoral clinical psychology students, with careful supervision (using videotapes) from qualified clinical psychologists. All sessions were of one and a half hours' duration. The IT format (after

Neimeyer 1988) involved therapists introducing a new dyadic disclosure topic each week (for example issues of trust, or of family secrets), increased levels of intimacy being implicated over the ten weeks in the topics chosen. Group members split into pairs to discuss the topic for four minutes, after which they would rotate prior to whole group discussion. The group process format was as described by Courtois (1988). Group members shared their goals and their incest histories in the first few sessions, after which the focus shifted to the individual's interactions with the group (as suggested by Yalom 1975). Thus, the actual topics raised were dictated by group members themselves. The researchers found that all groups showed improvement over time in terms of BDI scores (depression), though there were significantly greater improvements for both the treatment groups over the waiting list control. However, only the process groups showed a similar effect in social adjustment (SAS). In fact, waiting list controls actually deteriorated in this measure. In terms of general distress (SCL-90-R), both treatment groups improved, whereas control subjects showed no change. Changes were maintained at six-month follow-up, but several of the women requested further therapy.

Serrano (1989) provides a descriptive evaluation of a multi-modal arts therapy group. The group had two leaders, one a survivor of incest and one not, one a verbal therapist with an understanding of arts therapies and one an arts therapist with a working knowledge of psychotherapy. The group of six women met for twenty-five sessions lasting one and three-quarter hours. Serrano describes in some detail the structures used by the therapists, and the gradual progression of group members from victim to survivor. She concludes that therapists need to judge carefully which creative structures to use so as to maximise safety, dependent on the fragility of individual group members and the extent of previous therapy.

Campling and Culverwell (1990) decided to run a group for female survivors, in response to their National Health Service (NHS) contexts of a psychotherapy department with a twelve-month waiting list and a psychology department with a six-month waiting list. They planned a fourteen-session group programme, each session lasting one and a half hours. Crucially, assessments were coloured by the lack of alternatives, and it is possible that in the light of their experience they would have screened out some of the women. All of the women had been severely abused, from a young age, and over a long period. Several group members had been revictimised in some way, including currently abusive relationships. What emerged from this was that the abusive dynamics were replayed in the group.

Follette *et al.* (1991) attempted to find out what might predict a positive outcome for incest survivors in group treatment, using a similar methodology to that described above which was used by Alexander *et al.* (1989). Given that they recruited sixty-five women to their study via the media and mailings to therapists and that the authors of the two reports (Alexander *et al.* 1989; Follette *et al.* 1991) include some of the same people, it is possible that this was in fact the same set of subjects. Again, IT and group process groups were used, lasting for ten sessions of 90 minutes each, and facilitated by doctoral clinical psychology students using video-mediated supervision by experienced clinical psychologists who were also group therapists. The range of tests used was similar to that of Alexander *et al.* (1989). Follette *et al.* (1991) found that poorer treatment outcome was associated with less education; a history of oral-genital abuse or intercourse; higher levels of general distress as measured on the SCL-90-R and higher levels of depression as measured on Beck's inventory; and being currently married. They also found that, for group process therapy (which Alexander *et al.* 1989 found to be the more effective), previous individual therapy was predictive of a positive outcome. They conclude that previous individual therapy would be a useful adjunct to group therapy programmes with this client group, as would marital therapy.

Hunt and Bledin (1992) provide a response to Campling and Culverwell (1990), in their report of a time-limited (twelve-session), semi-structured group for women survivors. Their group was 'characterised by warmth and concern, a marked absence of competition and an ability to tolerate strong feelings of despair, hopelessness and anger' (Hunt and Bledin 1992, p.15). The single therapist (Hunt) used a feminist framework to guide her interventions. These included an eclectic mix of educative, supportive and semi-structured experiential approaches (including roleplay, use of art materials, bodywork and guided fantasy). She avoided dynamic interpretations but received clinical supervision from a psychoanalytically trained psychologist with experience of running groups for this client group. Hunt and Bledin (1992) found that the supportive and containing exercises were welcomed, especially a guided visualisation intended to develop control over personal space. A qualitative evaluation revealed that all of the women made some positive changes in their lives, but all of them felt that the programme was too short and that there had been little change in their experience of intimate relationships. Hunt and Bledin conclude that twenty sessions would be a more appropriate length for this kind of group. Interestingly, the group members perceived the single therapist as more like themselves, without the support of a second therapist. This identification with the therapist appears to have facilitated positive change. Campling and Culverwell (1990) found that in their group, which had all white members except one Asian woman, racism was one of the issues which emerged through which abuse dynamics were replayed; this issue never emerged in Hunt's all-white group.

Hazzard *et al.* (1993), like Follette *et al.* (1991), attempted to elicit the factors affecting group therapy outcome for CSA survivors. They provided year-long groups, each session lasting 90 minutes, for 148 women recruited via newspaper advertisements and therapist referrals; 92 per cent of the volunteers were Caucasian. The therapy was provided in a United States free service setting, the Georgia Council on Child Abuse. The therapists were either one or two in number for each group, masters or doctoral level mental health professionals, receiving expert supervision. The treatment model was based on Yalom's (1975) developmental model of group progression through formation of trust, integration of affect and building of skills, to separation and loss issues in the termination phase. Courtois (1988) provided the content. Volunteers for the research who were misusing substances, actively psychotic or suicidal, or otherwise exhibiting signs of extreme psychopathology were screened out. As with Follette *et al.* (1991), a pre- and post-test design was used, although without the benefit of a control group to aid interpretation of the results. The battery of tests used was somewhat different from that used by Follette *et al.*, although one commonality was the SCL-90-R. Other tests included the Trauma Symptom Checklist TSC-33 (Brière and Runtz 1989), the Locus of Control Scale (LOC) (Nowicki and Duke 1974), the Index of Self-Esteem (ISE) (Hudson 1982) and the Sexual Symptom Checklist (SSC) (Maltz and Holman 1987). Of these, the SSC had unknown reliability and validity. Unlike Follette *et al.* (1991), Hazzard *et al.* (1993) found no significant differences in outcome related to marital status, initial distress, or type of abuse. However, they did find that the more similar the group membership was in terms of type of abuse, the more likely the members were to display a positive outcome. The Caucasians also did better, which may be related to similarity issues as all the therapists were white and Caucasian participants were in the majority. Other indicators of a positive outcome included no history of previous drug misuse and having had previous therapy (the latter being consistent with Follette *et al.* 1991). Group completers were more likely not to have presented with a history of psychi-atric hospitalisations.

Fisher, Winnie and Ley (1993) examined the characteristics of drop-outs versus completers of a six-month group therapy programme for women who had a history of CSA. The sixty-four women were recruited from a larger sample of depressed women attending a community mental health centre in Canada. They found, using the Millon Clinical Multiaxial Inventory (MCMI) (Millon 1983), a scale based on DSM-III (American Psychiatric Association, 1980) that the completers had more overall psychopathology and that both groups of women met the criteria for borderline personality disorder. Both groups also had histories of revictimisation and poverty. However, the drop-outs were more likely to have been battered as children, to have been sexually abused solely within the family, and to be in relationships which were currently abusive with partners expressing hostility to the therapy.

Darongkamas *et al.* (1995) describe a British sixteen-session semi-struc-tured group therapy for survivors. Inclusion criteria were that each woman should feel positive about the therapy on offer; CSA was their primary concern for therapy; and there was currently some stability in their lives. Women were excluded if they were currently suffering psychotic symptoms. Post-group evaluation using their own questionnaire and a Belief Inventory (Jehu *et al.* 1988) showed some improvement in self-esteem and reduced self-blame, although some continued wariness concerning sexual relation-ships. Their evaluation also revealed the need for conjoint individual therapy.

Hall *et al.* (1995) evaluated a group analytic therapy programme via changes in depressive ratings and a measure of use of the primary care services. Ninety-four women survivors took part in six-month slow open groups. Ratings were made for up to seven years after leaving the group, using both Hamilton's (1967) and Beck's (1978) depression scales. Use of general practitioner services was recorded for up to five years. They found that both depression and service use measures decreased following the therapy, and were maintained for between two and seven years, the fall in depressive ratings being independent of anti-depressive medication. The patients themselves reported that change occurred in several other areas of their functioning.

Table 1.1 summarises some of the existing group therapy approaches for women survivors of CSA.

Table 1.1 – Group therapy for women CSA survivors

	No. therapists	No. sessions	Modality	Setting	Evaluation
Alexander et al. (1989)	2	10 (1½ hours)	interpersonal transaction (IT) vs group process	clinical psychology (USA)	improved depression, general distress, and social adjustment (latter in group process format only), but needed further therapy
Serrano (1989)	2	25 (1¾ hours)	creative multi-modal	community mental health centre (USA)	need care using some techniques with fragile groups
Campling and Culverwell (1990)	2	14 (1½ hours)	non-directive, dynamic verbal psychotherapy	NHS (no back-up) (UK)	abuse dynamics replayed in group
Follette et al. (1991)	2	10 (1½ hours)	IT and group process	clinical psychology (USA)	negative outcome associated with less education; history of oral-genital abuse or intercourse; more general distress and depression; currently married. For group process therapy, previous individual therapy helped
Hunt and Bledin (1992)	1 (2 planned)	12 (2 hours)	feminist, semi-structured, creative/multi-modal, not dynamic	NHS/social services 12-month early intervention project (UK)	supportive, containing experiences welcomed; 20 sessions would be better
Fisher et al. (1993)	1? (not explicit)	6 months (no session length stated)	not stated	community mental health centre (Canada)	drop-outs more likely to have been battered and CSA only within the family, also currently abused
Hazzard et al. (1993)	1 or 2	1 year (1½ hours)	process-orientated	free service (USA)	similarity, previous therapy and no history of drug misuse or hospitalisations all important
Darongkamas et al. (1995)	2	16 (1½ hours)	verbal discussion, semi-structured	NHS (UK)	self-esteem improved, less self-blame, though still wary of sexual relationships; need for therapy alongside group
Hall et al. (1995)	2 (1 male, 1 female)	up to 6 months (slow open) (1½ hours)	group analysis	NHS (UK)	depressive ratings, contacts with GP and with psychiatry all decreased; effect maintained 2–7 years

Recovery processes

There have been no systematic research studies concerning the process of recovery following chronic CSA trauma prior to my own (Meekums 1998) that I could find. There is, however, some degree of agreement between the different writers concerning the issues and themes which need to be addressed in any therapeutic intervention. Much of this is derived from Bass and Davis (1988), who propose fourteen stages of healing based on clinical experience. The stages are seemingly applicable whatever interventions are used: the decision to heal; the emergency stage; remembering; believing it happened; breaking silence; understanding that it was not your fault; making contact with the child within; trusting yourself; grieving and mourning; anger, the backbone of healing; disclosure and confrontations; forgiveness (which is not essential); spirituality; and resolution and moving on. Bass and Davis (1988) suggest that the recovery process is like a spiral. While Bass and Davis (1988) have been discredited in some circles for focusing on memory work, their description of the recovery process, based on clinical experience, is one of the clearest available in the literature so far.

Some writers (e.g. Herman 1992; Simonds 1994) argue that the recovery of memories is of central importance, while others (e.g. Berry 1997) warn against emphasising this process. Berry (1997) argues that there is little evidence that recovery of memories enhances recovery from the trauma of CSA. She also argues that abuse is only one of the formative experiences in a survivor's life and should not therefore be overemphasised. It is worth noting that the CSA of which Berry writes does not necessarily fall into the category of repeated trauma. Repeated CSA may be enforced through threats to the life of the victim or to others whom she loves. Herman (1992) suggests that this kind of experience might lead to what she calls 'complex post-traumatic stress disorder'. It is possible, if Herman's (1992) analysis is correct, that repeated CSA, perpetrated in childhood, has a profound effect on the developing sense of self. In contrast, a single incident from which the victim is enabled to recover through a loving, supportive and believing family may be traumatic but is less likely to injure the developing ego severely. All of the women participating in my own study apparently had histories of repeated CSA of the type which is likely, according to Herman (1992), to lead to 'complex post-traumatic stress disorder'. A conservative approach would be that as Jones (1991) suggests, it is the *relevant* account which needs to be told, which may not necessarily be the whole account of the abuse. In emphasising the 'relevant account', the survivor is encouraged to focus on her attributed meaning of events, rather than merely narrating a series of facts. It is generally accepted that the personal meaning of events is a key factor in defining whether or not they are perceived as traumatic.

Simonds (1994) offers a sequential approach to multi-modal therapy with CSA survivors, which is drawn from psychotherapy, art therapy and dance movement therapy approaches. She suggests: 'trauma resolution involves retrieval of traumatic memories accompanied by expression of affect. The ability to revisit the trauma leads to a realignment in the survivor's view of the world, the self, and others' (p.2).

Simonds (1994) cautions that this is usually long-term work, involving preparatory work before the survivor can face feelings and thoughts that have been hidden. She also cautions that the therapist must be aware of whether the survivor needs to work on containment, exploration or expression at any one time. To facilitate expression when the client needs to work on containment, she argues, could lead to a sense of being overwhelmed, resulting in possible setback or flight from therapy. Following the sequential three-phase model proposed by Herman (1992) and others, she suggests the following tasks in early, middle and late phase work:

1   The early phase sees the formation of the therapeutic alliance and creation of the conditions for safety and containment. This is also the phase during which an assessment is formulated, coping skills are developed, and realistic goals are agreed. There may be a need for crisis management.

2   In the middle phase, traumatic memories are accessed and connected to affect, slowly and carefully, so that new meanings can be elicited. This work may be interspersed with containing work from the early phase.

3   Resolution of the trauma involves a knowledge that the survivor was not to blame for the abuse and an ability to place the abuse in the past rather than confuse this with present events. The survivor can now work on here-and-now issues once more, for example relationship issues. She also faces the loss of the therapy and looks towards the future, possibly using consolidation strategies such as assertiveness training.

Herman (1992) suggests that group therapy may provide a particularly useful intervention for trauma survivors: 'Trauma isolates; the group re-creates a sense of belonging' (p.214). She refers to one of Yalom's (1975) curative factors associated with group psychotherapy, namely that of 'universality', or the sense that one is no longer alone. Speaking of her suggestion that there are three stages to recovery, Herman (1992) cautions the reader not to interpret these stages in a linear fashion: 'Oscillating and dialectical in nature, the traumatic syndromes defy any attempt to impose such simple-minded order' (p.155).

Herman (1992) reviews three pieces of research that appear to provide some evidence for the therapeutic effects of disclosure. The research she reviews indicates that telling the story of traumatic events, when this occurs in a safe therapeutic setting, has the effect of reducing symptoms associated with intrusion and hyperarousal. There is also some evidence that these effects are maintained at six months. The research cited is drawn from work with war veterans (Keane *et al.* 1989) and from a method used with Chilean victims of torture and mock executions (Cienfuegos and Monelli 1983) which was refined in Denmark with political refugees (Agger and Jensen 1990). However, Herman (1992) points out that, to obtain maximum effects, the methods described have to be repeated for each traumatic episode. She suggests a different approach for survivors of chronic trauma, involving the relating of key incidents which 'stand' for several incidents. Narration may be preceded by image-making, since Herman claims that traumatic memories are iconic in nature. My own view is that some traumatic memories may be at least partially encoded via sensori-motor experience, especially when they are from a very early stage of development. It would appear that Herman is mindful of this possibility, in fact, as she suggests that when telling the narrative it is important that the trauma survivor connects with feelings and bodily sensations in the presence of the therapist. The therapist facilitates this process, and helps the client to negotiate her way between past and present realities. Herman observes that, even after such treatment, the numbing and social effects will be unaltered, and that these require a relational approach to therapy. In order to address certain physiological effects of the trauma including alterations in sleeping, eating, pain perception, endocrine balance and psychosomatic disturbance, Herman suggests that specialist approaches may be necessary.

Table 1.2 summarises the models of recovery discussed in this section.

Table 1.2 – Models of recovery from CSA

	Modality	Pre-requisites	Starting point	Interim tasks	Goal	Form
Bass and Davis (1988)	self-help	decision to heal	varies	up to 12	resolution, moving on	spirallic
Herman (1992)	multi-modal	safety, therapeutic alliance	therapeutic relationship safety and containment	remembering, mourning, telling the story	resolution, reconnection, consolidation	three-phase, oscillating, marathon
Simonds (1994)	multi-modal	safety	therapeutic alliance coping skills	containment, exploration, expression	trauma resolution, preparing for future	three-phase, sequential

Therapeutic factors

While therapeutic factors have been studied in a wide range of approaches and contexts by previous researchers, my own research (Meekums 1998) does provide some new information regarding those involved in the recovery of women survivors of CSA in the context of a time-limited group arts therapies programme (GAT-P). I will discuss these in Chapter 3, when I present my model for recovery. Previous research has focused in individual therapy on the importance of the therapeutic alliance (Burns and Nolen-Hoeksema 1992; Rogers 1957; Truax and Carkhuff 1967) and other factors including therapist orientation, type of client and type of therapy (Mitchell et al. 1977). In the group situation, the therapeutic factors identified have included the instillation of hope; universality, that is the sense that one is not alone; the imparting of information; altruism; corrective recapitulation of the family of origin; the development of socialising techniques; imitative behaviour; interpersonal learning; group cohesiveness; catharsis; existential factors including an acceptance of what can and cannot be changed; and self-understanding (Yalom 1975). Bloch and Crouch (1987), apparently building on Yalom's work, reviewed more recent research concerning therapeutic factors in group psychotherapy which appears to indicate a particular relevance for the instillation of hope, group cohesiveness, altruism and universality.

Summary

In this chapter, I have reviewed the literature with respect to CSA. I have concluded that, not only is CSA an all-too-common phenomenon, but also it is more prevalent in the history of those people who use the psychotherapy and psychiatry services than in the general population, suggesting an aetiological role of CSA trauma in mental health disturbance. However, the research of Bagley (1995) in particular has shown that emotional abuse is more indicative of a poor mental health outcome than CSA alone, but that when emotional abuse is combined with a history of CSA the effects are more than doubled.

The topical issue of FMS has been discussed, and therapists are cautioned to be careful not to suggest a history of CSA on the basis of symptomotology alone, but to believe their clients in the interests of the therapeutic alliance, when they present with actual traumatic memories.

Theories of traumagenics are pertinent to treatment planning. I have discussed in particular the four traumagenics suggested by Finkelhor and Browne (1985): traumatic sexualisation, betrayal, stigmatisation and powerlessness. Herman's (1992) analysis of the three commonly reported clusters of symptoms (hyperarousal, intrusion and numbing) and the conceptualisation of these within a diagnostic framework of 'complex post-traumatic stress disorder' has also been found to be useful when planning treatment.

Existing treatment options have been briefly outlined, including group therapy studies, which together suggest a need for group therapy programmes to be organised within a wider support network such as exists within a properly executed care programme approach. In the British NHS, this ideally involves a key worker who co-ordinates a package of care for the individual client. The research studies examined here indicate the need for group therapy programmes to be organised around a twenty-session or six-month time-frame, and to make good use of supportive, containing structures in the interventions but to leave room for women's individual concerns to be aired.

Finally, theories of recovery have been reviewed, which show a remarkable lack of research in this area but some useful theoretical contributions based on clinical experience, in particular that of Herman (1992).

CHAPTER 2

Creative Approaches to Therapy:
Art Therapy, Dance Movement Therapy and Dramatherapy

Introduction

The creative arts therapies (CATs) (dramatherapy, dance movement therapy (DMT), art therapy and music therapy) each function within their own theoretical and practice frameworks, training in the UK being at postgraduate level. This book concerns itself with the three CATs which were available to my research (Meekums 1998). These were art therapy, DMT and dramatherapy. Definitions of each of the CATs vary; there is not a coherent definition of CATs that can be applied to all modalities. However, for the purposes of this book a unified definition is proposed: a creative arts therapy is the use of a specific art modality (e.g. dance movement, drama or art) within a therapeutic relationship.

There is some debate as to whether the CATs constitute discrete forms of psychotherapy, or whether they are distinct approaches to therapy in their own right. Jennings (1996), for example, argues strongly against identification with long-term psychotherapy, which she claims can disrupt family life as an individual forms a deep attachment to an outsider (the therapist). She also observes that the commitment to therapy can cause financial hardship. She goes on to say that long-term psychotherapy 'often robs the person of their own power and self-healing capacity' (p.202), creating unequal roles between therapist and client and blurring the boundaries between what she describes as 'everyday reality and dramatic reality' (p.202). In short, she believes that long-term psychotherapy 'takes over the person's life' (p.201) and advocates a 'move away from a problem-focused view of society' (p.213).

The debate among many arts therapists is often concerned with status: psychotherapists are considered to have greater status than either counsellors or arts therapists, as is reflected in their salaries in the British NHS mental health services and in private practice. Registration with the United Kingdom Council for Psychotherapy (UKCP) therefore would confer an air of respectability for arts therapists. The irony is that not all psychotherapists have specific training which would enable them to work with people who have enduring and complex mental health difficulties (Parry and Richardson 1996), whereas arts therapists in the NHS often do this kind of work. The Association for Dance Movement Therapy UK (ADMT (UK)) has fairly recently changed its definition to embrace the idea of DMT as a form of psychotherapy: 'Dance Movement Therapy is the psychotherapeutic use of movement and dance through which a person can engage creatively in a process to further their emotional, cognitive, physical and social integration' (*ADMT UK Quarterly* Spring 1997). It may be that, with government legislation to introduce a licence to practise for the Professions Supplementary to Medicine and the consequent formation of a council to administer this task (the Council for Professions Supplementary to Medicine or CPSM), organisations like the UKCP will become less important in conferring status to CATs practitioners than the CPSM.

Another debate often cited is whether or not the CATs are shamanistic. As West (1995), a healer and counsellor points out, this term is used rather loosely by practitioners from several disciplines, particularly on the west coast of the USA. Johnson (1988), an arts therapist, observes: 'Shamanism has in fact become a code word for anything that stirs passions or relates to the spiritual world – a use so broad that everything from psychotherapy to rock and roll is seen as shamanic' (p.270). Johnson suggests that in fact both the move for arts therapists to be seen as analysts and the identification with shamans are symptoms of the search for power.

Schmais (1988) attempts to draw out the differences between the CATs and shamanism. Briefly, these differences can be summarised thus:

- The shaman has a high status in the community, whereas the arts therapist's status is questionable.

- There are no time constraints in shamanistic ceremonies, unlike those characterising the typical 'therapy hour'.

- The arts therapist is more active than a psychoanalyst, but less active than a shaman in the healing process.

- Therapy is neither a sacred nor a significant event in the community.

- The kind of crisis typically endured by the shaman-initiate could be seen as encompassing a mental health breakdown potentially detrimental to postgraduate study.

- Shamans operate within a particular cultural framework, whereas arts therapists should strive to be sensitive to a wide range of cultural traditions.

Lewis (1988) poses an alternative view. She likens the transitional space (Winnicott 1971) to what she describes as 'the liminal space in shamanic healing' (Lewis 1988, p.310). This is the notional space in which the individual enters the place between internal and external reality, thus facilitating exploration of the client's personal symbolism. She also suggests that what dance movement therapists refer to as the 'somatic countertransference', in which the therapist feels in their body the projections of the client, is akin to the shaman's body being inhabited by spirits, a process which ultimately leads to transformation. Themes of letting go, of death and rebirth which are common in CATs practice, she claims, parallel the shamanic initiation process.

A consideration of the potentially shamanic dimension of the CATs is relevant to the topic of this book in that some writers, notably Bass and Davis (1988) and Kane (1989), have proposed a spiritual dimension to recovery from CSA. Kane (1989) describes a process similar to the shamanic journey: 'In reality, the woman needs her therapist to help her descend into her own body and to let her old self die' (p.35).

A third debate concerns whether or not creative arts therapists should be trained to use all modalities, as in person-centred expressive therapies for example. This debate links to the above concerning shamans, since the shaman is a master or mistress of several arts. However, the debate concerning specialism versus integration is by no means confined to the debate about shamanism. It is important to recognise this debate, since the treatment approach outlined in this book makes use of a multi-modal approach. Blatner (1991) hints at the possibility that the different CATs modalities can be used to good effect at different stages in the recovery process. He notes in particular the different degrees of distancing afforded by certain exercises, and suggests that therapists 'gradually work with their patients' defences to introduce experiences that produce and share more personal and emotionally meaningful material' (p.406). Blatner likens this process to the activity of play, during which one does not initially need to take full responsibility for the expression; in the context of safety, the client can gradually increase the level of insight involved in the process. In a similar vein to Jennings (1996), Blatner (1991) emphasises the role of the CATs in celebrating the healthy aspects of the individual rather than focusing solely on problem areas. Blatner seems to imply that this process can apply whichever modality is used. Blatner is himself a psychodramatist while Gorelick (1989), who draws the reader's attention to the central importance of metaphor in the CATs, is a poetry therapist, a profession which appears to have more recognition in the USA than in the UK. Gorelick admits to wishing he were expert in all of the CATs. He advocates a practice which maintains a central expertise in one modality while incorporating a level of competence in certain others.

The need for a range of modalities is also echoed by Levy (1992), who trained as both a dance movement therapist and psychodramatist. She advocates a multi-modal approach to psychotherapy which integrates these two disciplines into what she calls 'psychodramatic movement therapy' (p.191). Her method includes not only dramatic enactments and dance, but also drawing and visualisation. She justifies her approach in terms of the different needs of individuals to find expression through verbal, visual, physical or tactile routes. Levy suggests that any one individual may need different modalities at different times, starting with the one with which the person feels most comfortable. This eclecticism, also proposed by Minde (1993), herself an art therapist, would seem to be wise. A broad training, it could be argued, is particularly important in times of economic scarcity which do not allow most employers to set up departments with a full complement of arts therapists. It also allows for the preservation of the therapeutic relationship as container, during different stages of recovery.

Grainger (1990) advances the argument further, by proposing a common link between the CATs arising from their roots in art. Discussing the construction of meaning in art, he suggests: 'the process is essentially paradoxical. We distance ourselves (or art distances itself) in order to be engaged with, and involved in, the thing we are standing back from' (p.17).

Grainger (1990) suggests that this experience is common to all art forms, and that the end result of a creative act is a change in the self. The new self, he argues, sits alongside the old self, in relationship and dialogue. This results in a widening of personal boundaries. He concludes: 'a work of art challenges existing structures by its effort to engage human reality at a profounder level of perceptual clarity, that is, of meaning' (p.17).

Each of the CATs with which this book is concerned will now be considered briefly in turn. For the reader who wishes to know more about the individual arts therapies, a further reading list is given in Appendix 4.

Dance movement therapy

Dance movement therapy is the most recent of all the CATs to develop in Britain; full membership of the ADMT (UK) was available for the first time only in 1996. As the youngest of the CATs, DMT may have had to prove itself even more stringently than either dramatherapy or art therapy, as evidenced by the number of research studies employing a pseudo- experimental design. However, there could be another reason for this nervousness: dance has traditionally been associated with women who, suggests West (1995), himself a healer, therapist and counsellor, have been associated with pejorative statements to do with their intuitive capacities. The 'New Dance' movement of the 1970s began to challenge the images of women that had previously been portrayed in dance. Lansley (1977), for example, a former Royal Ballet dancer, found herself 'rebelling against the romantic images and roles that are projected in the ballet spectacle' (p.5). Lansley felt that the ballet tradition denied female dancers their own creativity. Ballet, claims Lansley, pressurised female dancers to conform to stereotypic images of women who were 'paid to "professionally" display our bodies as art/sex objects' (p.6), so that 'even on stage women have to disguise their strength and virtuosity behind airy fairy characters' (p.7). This often required both strength and extreme pain, observes Lansley. It is conceivable that, if female dancers are seen as 'airy fairy characters', dance movement therapists (most of whom are women) might be viewed similarly.

DMT is based upon the following five assumptions, as defined by Stanton-Jones (1992):

- Body and mind are in reciprocal interaction, so that a change in body movement will affect total functioning. (This point has been argued from a neurophysiological standpoint by Berrol 1992.)

- Movement reflects personality.

- The therapeutic relationship is central to the effectiveness of DMT. This is mediated by the therapist mirroring and responding to the client's movement.

- Movement can be evidence of unconscious processes in much the same way as squiggles, slips of the tongue and so on. Thus, movement can contain a symbolic function.

- The act of creating movement can be inherently therapeutic as it enables the client to experiment.

To this list, I would suggest that a sixth premise could be added:

- Since early object relations and dance movement are both characterised by holding, shaping, rhythm, synchronicity and reciprocity, one might conclude that there is a possibility for DMT to provide a vehicle for the recapitulation of the individual's ontological development (Meekums 1990).

Schmais (1985) has attempted to elicit what she considers to be eight curative factors in DMT. These are as follows:

- *Synchrony*, which is the existence of two events occurring at the same time. Synchrony is associated with empathic relating which echoes mother–child interaction (Condon and Sander 1974; Meekums 1990).

- *Expression*, which is symbolic, transformative and shared by the whole group.

- *Rhythm*, which assists organisation and reflects early experience.

- *Vitalisation*, which she suggests is linked to empowerment.

- *Integration*, which 'implies achieving a sense of unity within the individual and a sense of community between internal and external reality' (Schmais 1985, p.26). Integration, she suggests, is facilitated via the shared neuro-muscular pathways between movement and certain cognitive processes, allowing an interplay between felt experience and symbolic representation which can be validated by others in the group.

- *Cohesion*, which provides both the content and form of the dance and is communicated both rhythmically and spatially. Here Schmais makes an interesting observation: 'In dance therapy, contact through auditory and visual channels precedes touch, which is a reversal of the developmental process. For infants, touch is a means of developing trust, whereas for adults, if trust is lost, it must be regained before accepting touch' (Schmais 1985, p.30). I would suggest that this observation is particularly relevant when considering the context of CSA survivors.

- *Education*, which is the process of learning through one's own experience and through the experiences of others or via the therapist's interventions.

- *Symbolism*, which Schmais suggests is the least understood process in DMT, yet the most valuable: 'Rooted in dreams and nurtured in fantasy, symbols, in dance as in all art, abstract, abbreviate and structure what is seen, felt and imagined' (Schmais 1985, p.33).

Research studies suggest that DMT may be helpful in the following ways:

- reducing anxiety (Brooks and Stark 1989; Cruz and Sabers 1998; Kline *et al.* 1977; Kuettel 1982; Leste and Rust 1984; Low and Ritter 1998; Peterson and Cameron 1978; Ritter and Low 1996)

- correcting body image disturbances (Christrup 1962; May *et al.* 1974)

- improving self-concept (Puretz 1978)

- reducing depression (Brooks and Stark 1989; Kuettel 1982)

- developing positive mother–child relationships (Meekums 1988, 1990, 1991, 1992)

- assisting alcoholic women to develop their body-concept (Reiland 1990).

The overweighting of DMT research cited here is certainly likely to be due at least in part to my own bias as a dance movement therapist. However, there may be other factors at work. Since (as discussed above) dance has traditionally been seen as the least serious of the art forms and identified primarily with women, this may have contributed to dance movement therapists' attempts to prove themselves in the dominant culture of experimental research. This world has, until recently, been defined and dominated by men (Olesen 1994).

Dramatherapy

Jennings (1996), arguing for a brief approach to dramatherapy, claims that dramatherapy in this context: 'mobilises the healing power of the creative imagination, and that the aesthetic pull of dramatic form and structure in itself will restore a sense of equilibrium to the troubled person, by focusing on their artistic potential' (p.202).

Jennings maintains 'that the infant is born already dramatised' (p.206). She illustrates this point with reference to how mothers talk to their unborn children, investing them with the roles of confidant, friend or little monster. She also claims that dramatic reality is essential in the formation of hypotheses and that maturity involves the capacity to move in and out of dramatic reality.

Dramatherapy allows the client to view their issues through 'dramatic distancing' (Jennings 1993, p.18). As discussed above, Grainger (1990) proposes this as a general phenomenon of the arts which allows some emotional distance, while deepening the experience. This suggestion is echoed by Jennings (1993): 'It is a complex process and engages the participant or viewer in multiple layers of experience, rather than in the unilinear dimension implied by "distance and closeness"' (p.18).

Jennings explains the process further: 'Through the theatre convention, we allow time and distance to be compressed or speeded up, we experience a selected number of events within a scene, and we react "as if" we are receiving the truth' (p.19).

Landy (1996) also points out that dramatherapists use projective techniques, for example puppetry and masks, which 'imply a projection of the self and thus, a certain kind of intrapsychic and interpersonal distancing' (p.14).

The processes leading to performance, and the theatre art itself, claims Jennings (1993), are at the very core of dramatherapy practice, the aim being to create new insights, experiences and perspectives about the world and one's relationship to it. Grainger (1990) suggests that in addition to the metaphorical truthfulness of the play, there is an equally important contrast between the form of the play (with a beginning, middle and end) and 'the shapelessness of life as we ourselves are conscious of actually being in the process of experiencing it' (p.20).

This ability to form and shape experience, and thus to contain it, it could be argued, is a feature of all of the arts. As with all forms of therapy, Grainger suggests that it is the act of reaching out to others and sharing in this case the drama that makes it healing. He also suggests that: 'The most important thing of all about drama is that it allows us to revise the way we look at life' (p.26).

Jones (1996) has identified nine core processes in dramatherapy which are, he claims, 'fundamental processes within all Dramatherapy' (p.99), rather than techniques.

- *Dramatic projection.* This is defined as 'the process by which clients project aspects of themselves or their experience into theatrical or dramatic materials or into enactment, and thereby externalise inner conflicts' (p.101).

- *Therapeutic performance process.* This 'involves the process of identifying a need to express a particular problematic issue, followed by an arrival at an expression of that issue which uses drama in some way' (p.103).

- *Dramatic empathy and distancing.* Jones suggests: 'The functions of empathy and distancing within Dramatherapy are related but different for 'actor' and for 'audience member' (p.106). He also suggests that both processes are likely to exist for the client during any piece of work, and that it is this dynamic which may create change. For example, in the transition from playing a part to de-roling, clients may change their perspective on the role or on the situation which has been explored.

- *Personification and impersonation.* Personification involves 'using objects (e.g. toys or puppets) to represent material' (p.108). Impersonation involves 'depicting something or playing a part themselves' (p.108).

- *Interactive audience and witnessing.* Witnessing 'is the act of being an audience to others or to oneself within Dramatherapy. Both aspects are of equal importance' (p.112). The audience is interactive, and within any one session a client may employ both performer and audience roles.

- *Embodiment.* This 'concerns the way a client physically expresses and encounters material in the "here and now" of dramatic presentation' (p.114). This process, claims Jones, deepens the encounter and so 'the use of the body in Dramatherapy is crucial to the intensity and nature of a client's involvement' (p.114). Jones suggests that embodiment within dramatherapy can enable clients who have experienced traumatic incidents related to the body, to explore these issues.

- *Playing.* This enables an experimental attitude towards oneself and one's experiences. This may include projective work with objects and toys, in addition to the use of the body in play, and can provide a developmental continuum, for example from solitary to co-operative play.

- *Life–drama connection.* This refers to the possibility of enacting real-life situations on the one hand, or mythical and even abstract performance-related material on the other hand. It also refers to the possibility that, in being involved in another client's drama, links may be made to one's own experience. Jones points out the need for clarifying the 'make believe' aspects of drama for those clients whose hold on reality is tenuous.

- *Transformation.* Jones refers here to the way in which life experiences, people and objects can be transformed into their symbolic representations. He also refers to the process of personal change through the experimental nature of, for example, improvisation.

Dramatherapy research is more sparse than that in DMT, although Mackay *et al.s* (1987) study addresses the CSA context and is reviewed on pp.63–64.

Art therapy

British art therapy has developed within a strong psychodynamic framework, originally having reference to the work of Jung and later to Winnicott and Klein (Case and Dalley 1990). Important concepts have included symbol formation, object relations, play and the inner world of the individual (Case and Dalley 1990). It could be argued that these are fundamental processes to all CATs. However, Dubowski (1990) points out that iconic and linguistic development are initially separate in the child, and only later integrated. This would lend some theoretical support for the use of art therapy in accessing early experience and bypassing cognitive (left brain) processes. Rabiger (1990) proposes the idea of art therapy as a container, an idea which I have personally seen used by art therapy colleagues. Containment arises, at least in part, from the physical projection of images onto paper (see also Waller and Dalley 1992). These images arise from the unconscious, and may elude verbal articulation. Once projected and contained by the paper, the images can be worked with (for example torn or otherwise destroyed), or can be left in the knowledge that they can be returned to at the right time (Minde 1993). At this stage, the image can be added to, in order to present and explore further possibilities. Dalley (1997) also suggests that the art object can provide a focus for discussion and a mediator in the relationship between therapist and client.

Waller and Dalley (1992) suggest that the term 'art therapy' 'is a term which has been used to describe a collection of diverse practices, held together fundamentally by their practitioners' belief in the healing value of image-making' (p.3).

As with the other CATs, the degree to which practitioners view themselves as psychotherapists appears to vary. Birtchnell (1984) provides an early account of this debate:

> There are those who argue that the art therapist is essentially a trained artist who does therapy and those who argue that he is essentially a trained psychotherapist who uses art... To my mind, the art component of art therapy is very much subsidiary to the therapy one (p.30).

More recently, some of the courses which train art therapists have begun to define the profession as 'art psychotherapy'.

There is some research to suggest that behaviour disordered children can increase their control through participation in art therapy groups (Rosal 1993), but Hagood (1990) concludes that much research in art therapy is poorly designed and anecdotal or case-study based, allowing for few inferences concerning its efficacy.

The role of metaphor in creative arts therapies

Gorelick (1989) suggests that the uniting force behind the CATs is their use of metaphor, which provides a way of communicating complex human experiences without the need for long and often inadequate descriptions. Metaphor enables the conveyance of the essence of a complex experience with simplicity and without losing any of its richness, thus making the experience understandable to others (Billow 1977). In the CATs, metaphor provides 'a way into a closed situation' (Jones 1996) and may be used either in the linguistic sense, or in movement, painting, drama and the structuring of space. Thus a gesture can express feeling; a painting, drama or poem can tell a story; and the structuring of space can say much about the person's relationships. Metaphor, by its very nature, can be used to explore alternative ways of thinking and behaving (Lakoff and Johnson 1980). So, an image of help can be imported into a picture, a gesture can change from pushing to reaching, relationships can be redefined by using space differently, and a drama or poem can be reconstructed to bring hope into present reality. Cox and Theilgaard (1987) use the term 'mutative metaphor' to describe the use of metaphor to induce change, while Gendlin (1962) suggests that experience changes as it is symbolised. Grenadier (1995) suggests a subtle approach to her work as a music therapist and expressive therapist, allowing the images created by the client to speak for themselves and avoiding interpretation.

The use of metaphor in therapy is not confined to CATs: Sledge (1977) writes about the use of linguistic metaphors in psychoanalytic psychotherapy; Milner (1952) concerns herself with symbolism (a category which includes metaphor) in psychoanalytic psychotherapy. Angus and Rennie (1989) suggest that the use of metaphor is intrinsic to verbal psychotherapy. They claim that its function is threefold: to provide associative links with other areas of meaning; to reflect issues of self-identity; and to provide a representation of role-relationship patterns used by the client. This information was generated by Angus and Rennie (1989) via a qualitative inquiry. They audiotaped single therapy sessions with five clients, then played back the tapes to both client and therapist independently, to elicit their recollections of the use of metaphor. In a later study, Rennie (1994) used a similar methodology with fourteen therapy clients, to elicit the role played by storytelling in therapy. He concluded that storytelling aids distance from inner disturbance while simultaneously drawing attention to it, thus facilitating exploration either openly in the session or privately by the client. This point has been explored further by McLeod (1996): he discusses the emergence of 'narrative' perspectives in counselling and psychotherapy, suggesting that the task of the counsellor is to assist the client in 're-authoring' their life story.

Winnicott (1971) has written at some length about the importance of symbolic play in psychoanalytic psychotherapy with children. The discipline of play therapy as practised by Axline (1964) and others is based on the importance of children's symbolic play as a means of communication and of 'working through' issues and feelings. In these instances, much of the symbolism used by children is metaphoric, rather than concrete as in the use of a word as a symbol for an object.

The word 'metaphor' comes from the Greek words *meta* and *phora*, meaning to carry across. Several writers have pointed out that the word 'transference' as used in the therapeutic relationship has the same meaning, coming from the Latin *trans* and *fereo*. Metaphor, it has been suggested, can act both to distance the client from the emotional content of its reference, and to reduce the distance between client and therapist (Angus and Rennie 1989;

Cox and Theilgaard 1987; Sledge 1977). Sledge likens this deepened communication between client and therapist to wordless communication, and suggests that metaphor can function as a way of expressing something which might otherwise be inexpressible. Cox and Theilgaard (1987) claim that, since overwhelming emotions are contained via the metaphor, the client can begin to access through metaphor, experiences that have been suppressed in the unconscious. Shuttleworth (1985) adds that uncomfortable topics can, through the use of metaphor, be addressed comfortably and even with humour. Shuttleworth proposes that the power in metaphor lies in its ability to evoke that which is unconscious and mediated through right brain activity, and that to draw attention to the meaning of the metaphor through intellectual processes (left brain activity) would reduce its power. This is slightly different from Cox and Theilgaard's (1987) suggestion that metaphor bridges left brain and right brain activity, or conscious and unconscious processes. Cox and Theilgaard's suggestion links most fully with theories of the creative process (discussed below). Billow (1977), reviewing the psychological literature concerning metaphor, notes that metaphoric images contain sensory references. He also states that the use of metaphor is more difficult for people who are brain damaged or suffering from what is usually diagnosed as schizophrenia; people with these diagnoses may tend to take the metaphoric literally and vice versa. The nature of metaphor is such, he says, that not only can a metaphor contain multiple meanings and contexts, but also it may create a new concept for which there is no other expression. Metaphor can also be used to aid memory due to its inherent associative links.

The creative process in therapy

In order to examine the role of the creative process in therapy, it is necessary to look both within and outside the theory relating to CATs. I have previously made a case for seeing the research process as a creative process (Meekums 1993). Since creativity theory links discovery and creation in both the arts and sciences (see e.g. Boden 1990; Gordon 1975; Koestler 1964; Tardif and Sternberg 1988), it is reasonable to hypothesise that the same process might be identified in several different spheres of action. It may be, for example, that management processes, decision-making processes and therapeutic processes could all be viewed as creative processes.

The creative process can be conceptualised in four stages (Boden 1990; Gordon 1975; Hadamard 1954; Meekums 1993; Poincaré 1982):

1   *Preparation or striving*, during which the creator works hard at the task, and may feel frustrated, as if little is being achieved.

2   *Incubation*, during which the creator consciously lets go of the process, for example by taking a walk, although much unconscious work is potentially carried out.

3   *Illumination*, during which insights and connections are made.

4   *Verification*, which is essential since not all insights are useful in the long term.

Blatt (1991) has attempted to explain DMT in these terms although her definitions of each of the four stages differ slightly from those employed by myself both here and elsewhere (Meekums 1993, 1998).

In a previous work (Meekums 1993), I suggested that the creative process is essentially a rhythmic interchange between action and stillness. A similar point has been made by May (1975), who writes of the 'necessity of *alternating work and relaxation*' (p.66, original emphasis). This rhythmic process may also be alluded to by McLeod (1990) when he suggests that the middle phase of counselling is characterised by 'a rhythm of immersion in self followed by reflection' (p.12). It is at times of withdrawal from outward striving that insights occur, yet the initial striving is important and necessary. Some writers, for example Capra (1976) and Fox (1983), have developed ideas linking the creative process to a mystical experience. I have pointed out that there are similarities between the accounts of people working in seemingly unconnected spheres (Meekums 1993), for example the dancer Fulkerson (1982) writing about the creative process in dance, the Zen master Suzuki (1973) writing about Zen practice, and the child psychiatrist Winnicott (1965), writing about mother–infant interaction. In all of these, there appears to be a rhythmic alternation between active engagement and a letting go which does not imply a loss of continuity in the process.

In any creative process, it is likely that more than one point of insight will be necessary. It is therefore reasonable to view the creative process as a spiral (Meekums 1993), a process of forming during which the first vague urges to create become increasingly clarified. I have previously drawn the analogy of approaching a form in the fog (Meekums 1993); at certain times the form may look like something completely different, until the Gestalt clarifies. Gordon (1975) has likened the not-knowing often experienced in therapy to the process of incubation, and has emphasised the importance of being able to tolerate this stage. I would suggest that it may be, in fact, that the not-knowing is revisited many times if therapy is a creative spiral, and that each moment of illumination gives only part of, or even an inaccurate picture of, the eventual form which is being created or discovered. Aldridge, Brandt and Wohler (1990) have suggested that the introduction of form and order enables the client to become more whole, to escape fragmentation. They make the distinction between creative expression and cathartic expression, the latter lacking this sense of forming and integration unless it occurs within the context of the former.

Winnicott (1971) has linked the creative process to play, during which inner reality is brought to bear on external reality. For the child, play occurs in the potential space between mother and child. If this is so, and given that the therapy relationship can be viewed as transferential, in which the therapist often represents important figures in the client's life including the mother, the therapeutic creative process can be viewed as occurring in the potential space between client and therapist. This view would tend to support the notion that the therapeutic process is essentially a co-creational one, to which both client and therapist contribute. Since play, according to Winnicott, is an activity during which the self is recreated, therapy may also provide a way of recreating the self. I have suggested (Meekums 1993), with reference to T.S. Eliot and others, that in this potential space, time and space do not exist as they do in concrete reality. Memories, dreams, fantasies and present external reality can mix and merge, and all become accessible in the here and now. Yet the creative process implies a benevolent presence (Fulkerson 1982; Winnicott 1965), enabling the client to confront and explore potentially frightening material within the container of creativity.

The creative arts therapies and child sexual abuse

I would like to propose that the CATs, because of their emphasis on metaphor, might be a particularly useful tool in therapy for people who have been sexually abused as children. The rationale I am using is as follows:

- given that survivors of CSA who present in the mental health services are likely to have suffered repeated and multiple forms of abuse (Bagley 1995) and will therefore bring complex issues to be addressed within therapy, metaphor might provide ways to address some of this complexity

- the survivor may have no words for what happened, since the memories are linked often to very early developmental stages

- the abuse may have interrupted education to the extent that verbal expression is difficult in general

- memories may be too painful to utter verbally

- the survivor may have considerably developed verbal skills which may be used as a defence against feeling

- since the severe traumata are relatively rare, colloquial language does not contain the expressions which might adequately describe experience (Byrd 1995).

None of these problems entirely precludes the use of verbally-based psycho-therapeutic approaches. Simonds (1994) cautions that CATs may not be appropriate for everybody, but in certain circumstances they may provide a useful alternative or addition to verbal psychotherapy. As I have discussed above, the creative process is thought to make use of what Winnicott (1971) called the 'potential space' between inner and outer reality, conscious and unconscious, thus bridging these two worlds. The CATs may therefore be useful in accessing deeply buried memories and feelings. It is in this respect that the therapist needs to be aware both of the power inherent, and the possible caution needed in applying CATs techniques. If one accepts the suggestion that the CATs may access deeply unconscious material, then it is possible that the CATs may access memories in a way for which the client is unprepared. A previously relatively intact survival mechanism may be shattered by what emerges unless there is an infrastructure to support the survivor through the process. Furthermore, it is important that the therapist does not attempt in any way to influence the nature of disclosures, to avoid eliciting false memories. Yet the process is an essentially collaborative one. This presents a dilemma for the practitioner: there is a need to preserve the collaborative, co-creational aspects of the work since this enables clients to feel safe in the knowledge that their therapist is alongside them. Yet, the memories must be those of the survivor, uncontaminated by the therapist's preconceptions. The problems in a group setting might be even greater, it could be argued.

There are two ways to overcome this dilemma, once it is recognised. The first is the rigorous use of clinical supervision, in which therapists reflect on the impact of the work on them, and on how they might be influencing their clients. The second is the knowledge that, in the absence of litigation, verification of memories is not an issue since the psychotherapist works with the client's truth (Fonagy and Target 1995). It behoves the therapist to be vigilant to the possibility of a history of abuse in any client seeking help, while working with the actual experience of these clients and their own expressed needs. These needs may be for disclosure (as in the more exploratory therapies), for more adaptive coping strategies (as for example in cognitive/behavioural therapy) or for control of symptoms (as for example in drug treatments). Therapeutic needs can, of course, change over time. The CATs can be focused to each of the goals of exploration, coping strategies and symptomatic control.

There are several descriptive accounts of CATs in the treatment of CSA survivors, but very few research studies. Simonds (1994) describes a multi-modal approach to working with survivors, emphasising the integration of art and movement techniques into verbal psychotherapy. Serrano (1989) uses a wider range of creative techniques including roleplay, bodywork, visualisation, drawing and sculpting.

Ambra (1995) interviewed five San Francisco Bay area dance movement therapists about their work with adult CSA survivors. She found that issues of assertiveness, body image, sexuality and boundaries were common themes. The therapists also stressed the need to address issues of safety, trust and shame. Comments were largely positive concerning the usefulness of the modality. This may reflect a bias in the style of questioning, or in the sample which included private practitioners who perhaps worked with clients whose symptomatology was not severe. Geographical influences may also have created a sample bias.

Mackay et al. (1987) present one of the few research studies in dramatherapy, and one of the few in the use of CATs with survivors of CSA. They report a pilot study with five girls aged 12–18, who met for eight weekly dramatherapy sessions, each lasting four to five hours. A range of valid and reliable scales including Beck's Depression Inventory (BDI) (Beck 1978) and the SCL-90 (Derogatis, Lipman and Covi 1973) were used both at the start of the first session and part-way through the final session. These tests were administered by one of the authors who was not one of the therapists. They found that levels of depression, hostility and psychotic thinking decreased significantly, and there was a non-significant increase in self-esteem, although the authors acknowledge that the small sample makes interpretation difficult. Mackay et al. (1987) also did not use a control group, the addition of which would have given a more accurate picture of the significance of any pre- to post-test changes.

Levens (1994), an art therapist and psychodramatist, describes the now controversial use of guided imagery with survivors of CSA. In the light of Loftus' (1994) remarks (see the section on false memory syndrome, Chapter 1) it is important to note that Levens (1994) gives the reader a seemingly verbatim account of her use of a guided fantasy. At no stage does she suggest directly that the participant has been abused. The narrative suggests various open-ended scenarios, and the participants are invited to make images from what they experience. The context was a British eating disorders unit, and all members of the group at that time had already disclosed CSA, the perpetrator in each case being a father-figure. Interestingly, far from finding that the participants were very suggestible, Levens (1994) noted that some of the participants reacted negatively to the form of guided imagery, experiencing it as controlling.

Three other art therapists give different examples of how art therapy might be used with adult survivors of CSA: Anderson (1995) uses clay for both catharsis and empowerment; while Brooke (1995a) uses the more traditional medium of marks on paper; and Nez (1991) integrates both drawing and clay work in his case study of individual therapy with a woman who had suffered physical and emotional abuse and suspected sexual abuse, in the absence of actual CSA memories. Nez (1991) frames the client's work within the container of the myth of Persephone, and describes the client's growing sense through the art therapy that she no longer needed to explore the past. Anderson (1995) reports a naturalistic evaluation study of a nine-week clay therapy group programme. All participants reported at follow-up that the therapy group had been significant or very significant in their lives, and most of their therapists reported that the clients' self-esteem had improved. Anderson suggests that nine sessions is too short an intervention, and that ongoing individual therapy and other sources of personal support are essential to maximise positive effects. Brooke (1995a) gives an account of a more traditional research study to determine effects on self-esteem. She employed the Culture-Free Self-Esteem Inventory (Battle 1981; Brooke 1995b), a valid and reliable scale, studying an experimental group of six women who attended an eight-session art therapy group and a waiting-list control group of five women. Brooke (1995a) found moderate improvements in self-esteem for the experimental group, particularly on the general and social self-esteem scores, although personal self-esteem remained low. The start scores of the two groups were dissimilar, the experimental group having lower self-esteem. The improvements meant that the end scores of the two groups became similar. Brooke suggests that personal self-esteem might be better addressed through individual therapy.

Summary

In this chapter, I examined ways of conceptualising the CATs. This has included a consideration of the CATs as possible psychotherapies, shamanistic activities and integrative approaches. I briefly reviewed the theoretical writings on each of the CATs. I then outlined some of the core attributes of the CATs, including the role of the creative process and the use of metaphor, and considered their usefulness in the light of the FMS debate. I argued that the creative process is central to the therapeutic process, and that metaphor provides a unique opportunity for the recovery from the trauma of CSA. I also examined some of the sparse research evidence to support the suggestion that the CATs may play a role in treatment planning for CSA trauma survivors.

CHAPTER 3

A Creative Model for Recovery from CSA Trauma

Introduction

In this chapter I discuss the model for recovery from CSA developed during my doctoral research (Meekums 1998). The research involved a participative inquiry with fourteen women, each of whom had taken part in one of four twenty-session multi-modal arts therapy groups for survivors of child sexual abuse in an adult mental health setting. Each group was co-facilitated by two creative arts therapists. The therapists were qualified in DMT, dramatherapy or art therapy. I was involved clinically in three out of the four groups, but removed from this role for the final group. This enabled me to compare the role of researcher with that of researcher-practitioner. Space does not allow me to enter into any discussion regarding the different roles here, but in general the effects of my clinical involvement on the research and vice versa were positive. The validity of findings was aided by a reflexive and participatory approach to research and by the rigorous use of both clinical and academic supervision.

The methodology for the research is described in some detail in Appendix 1. Data collection was via semi-structured interviews, which were then analysed via a coding system. Preliminary conclusions were checked and refined in consultation with research participants. The model of recovery I present here was refined via selective reanalysis of all fourteen interviews.

The theoretical model developed must be viewed as provisional, a 'convenient fiction' (Herman 1992, p.155). It is important to appreciate that this is inevitably an oversimplification of a very complex process. The recovery process is not a neatly followed series of events but may represent overlapping phenomena. In reality, recovery is neither smooth nor predictable. On the contrary, recovery is long, painful, often unpredictable, marred by apparent setbacks and relieved by occasionally joyous moments. It is usually only with hindsight that progress can be evaluated, making positivist outcome research difficult. However, I hope that my model may help clients and therapists alike to make sense of the journey of recovery. The model conceptualises the recovery process as spirallic in nature, so that certain tasks are revisited several times but from an augmented perspective, with an overall tendency towards integration. Apparent setbacks, in which the client feels as if she is revisiting old material, may simply represent the corresponding point on the turn of a spiral, but at a different level. This provides one explanation for the need continuously to address the client's sense of safety for example, and to revisit important themes and issues several times. The spirallic process is essentially a creative process, marked by striving, incubation, illumination and verification (see Chapter 2 for a fuller discussion of the creative process) and leading to an overall forming and shaping of the self.

My epistemological stance in conducting the research was that the women who participated are the authorities regarding their own experience. The central importance of the research participants' own words in generating the theoretical model presented in this chapter is thus reflected in extensive quotations from the interviews.

Vector catalysts

Introduction to vector catalysts

Some of the tasks of recovery, in particular the establishment of safety, letting go into the art form and witnessing by the group, appear to facilitate other aspects of the recovery process. These therapeutic factors, while affecting the recovery process as a whole, are revisited at key points in the overall process, and thus are therapeutic tasks in their own right. However, to distinguish them from the other tasks of recovery, I have chosen the term vector catalysts to describe those factors which can make therapeutic interventions either helpful when present, or destructive when absent.[1] Of the three factors identified as facilitating the other tasks of recovery, I would suggest that a sense of safety and its related task of witnessing and being witnessed come into the category of vector catalyst. Immersion in the arts activity, however, is a catalyst to the process but does not appear to influence negatively the direction of recovery by its absence and does not therefore warrant the title of vector catalyst. I shall now separately consider each of the vector catalysts in turn.

A sense of safety

The need for safety was the single most often referred to element in recovery by all fourteen research participants in my study. There is also evidence in the existing literature for the importance of establishing a sense of safety in any therapeutic intervention. Writers and researchers have for some time emphasised the importance of the therapeutic relationship and of group cohesion in facilitating the therapeutic process (Rogers 1957; Yalom 1975). When the group is cohesive and the relationship with a therapist warm and genuine, empathic and conveying a sense of being understood, it is not difficult to see that the client can feel safe.

But even trusting other survivors can be difficult, as this research participant's words testify:

> [It was difficult]…trying to convince myself that nobody here was going to hurt me… Even when you trust the people and you know you are safe, when you're living through something so horrific it's very hard to reassure yourself.

This statement is an important one; it illustrates the sense of struggle (see pp.82–85). It also alludes to the sense echoed by several of the research participants, that in the early stages of recovery memories are felt to be present as if the abuse were happening now. It is as if the adult is no longer an adult who knows she is safe but has become again the abused child, and is reliving her experience of abuse.

During a particular session of one GAT-P, there was a sense that the therapy group was not a cohesive whole, but a series of fragments, each engaged in a different activity. This was disconcerting for one woman, who like several of the research participants placed particular value on group cohesion.

Another woman noticed that the women in her group, while trying to achieve cohesion, were also 'all trying to stay in our own little corner'. She felt that there was much more tension in this group than in previous therapy groups she had attended, as if it was more difficult to dissolve the barriers between people.

Unfortunately, in such a precarious situation some betrayal of trust may even be more likely; at least two of the GAT-Ps suffered crises of trust which appear to have been in some way experienced as replication of the abuse. This experience echoes that of Campling and Culverwell's (1990) group (see Chapter 1).

Therapists often shy away from accepting that their interventions can lead to deterioration in a client's mental state, but Lambert, Bergin and Collins (1977) have provided us with a useful overview of the factors associated with deterioration following group psychotherapy. These include encouragement of confrontation; expressions of anger; rejection by the group leader; feedback overload; coercive group norms for participation; low self-esteem; poor interpersonal skills; and mental health symptom severity. I would argue that this list of factors contributing to deterioration can also be viewed as relating to the client's level of perceived safety.

In my research study, certain interventions in the absence of a sense of safety appeared to have an effect towards deterioration, not merely a slowing of the recovery process. Moreover, safety could be threatened at any stage in the therapy.

The interventions which tended to be harmful in the absence of the required level of perceived safety tended to be those which led to increased awareness and disclosure of details surrounding the abuse. Yet, when the required safety was present, these same interventions could be positively transforming.

A sense of safety was generated in the following ways, as identified by the research participants:

- Group agreements: some women had concerns about confidentiality which they expressed at assessment. These were addressed by the group therapists' usual procedure of establishing a confidentiality rule within the group.

- The therapists encouraged an atmosphere in which individual differences between group members were valued rather than judged. This led to a sense of trust, of being understood and of being valued despite differences, which seems to link with Yalom's (1975) 'group cohesiveness'.

- The sharing of concerns and of previously held secrets led to a sense that the survivor was no longer alone, that experience was shared. This is what Yalom (1975) refers to as 'universality'. One of the ways in which the group situation can be especially effective, when it works well, is in providing concrete evidence that there are others who have suffered and survived in similar ways. This fact links to the part of the recovery process which I describe as witnessing (see pp.76–80). Several of the women spoke of the comfort of looking back on the group programme and remembering the other women:

> but it's that strength from the group ... that's probably helping me to cope with this ... I've had the 'comfort' in looking back to group sessions, that I wasn't on my own.

- The heterogeneity of the group meant that it was possible to witness others at different stages in their recovery. This led for some women to the 'instillation of hope' (Yalom 1975).

- Through witnessing others, several women gained an increased understanding of the powerlessness of the abused child, leading to a reduced sense of guilt. This appears to link with Yalom's (1975) 'self-understanding'.

- Careful timing of interventions, so that containing, group-building interventions were emphasised before the more exploratory and expressive techniques. Several research participants referred to the need for time in the programme to establish trust between group members before being led towards the exploration of painful issues. It was also important to check out whether group members were ready to witness a piece of work; one participant felt upset and troubled by seeing other women expressing their anger cathartically. The timing of activities was an important aspect of the therapists' role, as discussed below with regard to the dilemma of embodiment (see pp.88–92). For example, one woman had felt angry with the therapists when engaged in a group movement activity in which a ball was bounced on a stretch cloth. She later realised that this was due to a symbolic association with painful memories. When I asked her about the timing of this activity, she said that if it had occurred later in the group:

> I think I could have accepted it, and not been angry doing it. But what I wanted to do was just to let the thing go. Not run out, but come and sit back over here, but that wouldn't have been fair to eight other people. It's like a chain. The link would have been broken then ... we were there as a group, supporting each other, so I wouldn't have been fair on the other members by doing that. Because, if you've got a piece of cloth and you're shaking it like we were doing, and then you've got two people instead of three, well it's not going to work for them.

- The length of sessions and of the GAT-P. The length of each session and of the programme as a whole was one problem area in establishing safety; several participants would have liked longer, in order to feel safe enough to open up (speak: pp.97–100) without the threat that this would leave them having to cope alone with painful feelings:

> how would I feel, you know, by exposing these words, by actually coming out with something? Would I be controllable? Would I be able to cope?

Several of the survivors had been abused over a long period, by more than one person. This led to a sense that the GAT-P was not long enough to deal with each memory or group of memories (see Herman 1992). The element of timing in facing (p.96) certain issues was an important factor in establishing safety. At least one woman discovered that she was more likely either to bury (pp.85–87) or to feel overwhelmed by her feelings when confronting painful issues if this occurred early in the programme. While it was possible to respond to these comments by increasing the length of each session from one and a half hours to two hours in the next GAT-P, it was decided not to increase the length of the programme itself. Instead, assessment criteria were modified so that very vulnerable women did not enter into time-limited group therapy until they had had experience of disclosure with an individual therapist.

- The use of humour. Shuttleworth (1985) refers to the use of humour in therapy, as a way of providing safe distance from difficult material. One woman remarked that the use of humour gave her a break from the tension she experienced in facing the reality of the abuse.

- Emphasising each woman's right to say 'no' to participation in a suggested activity. This enabled at least some group members, it seems, to experience themselves as adults rather than as victimised children:

> Being able to say no and be heard was a big plus. Not having to go along with what everybody else was doing, and being respected for saying no. Being given a chance to be in control

of a situation – for once in my life not being made to feel under pressure.

They didn't just say you do this, you do that, you had a choice. You weren't made to do anything... Because I'd been ordered about all my life...and it was nice to be treated like an adult with a brain.

Paradoxically, the freedom to disclose only what she felt ready to disclose enabled at least one woman to do so more easily.

- It was also felt to be essential that the therapists structured the process, in order to make it feel safe and controlled. One woman felt that the physicality of the movement structures enabled her to come 'right down to earth if you've only got an image in your mind'. However, she was not advocating rigidity. The mix implied is subtle and requires skill on the part of the therapists:

> I would say that the whole thing is so gently done that – the knowledge of structure is there. Obviously it's got to be, and discipline, and a certain routine, but it's not obvious. It's very, very, very unobvious...very empathic without being oppressive, you know. There's actually no feeling of being pushed in a particular direction or rushed into something ahead of time, you know?

The delicate balance between freedom and structure seems also to have linked for at least one woman with her sense that she was not being judged by others. This enabled her to give herself permission to be creative, to trust her own impulses:

> ...nobody was judged by anybody. Including the girls, nobody judged. There was the opportunity to be heard, nothing was rushed. If you wanted to take time talking about it, then you were given the opportunity to talk about it. I mean, I suppose you had some sort of plan as to what we were going to do but it wasn't a rigid plan. It could be altered, it could fit in with us depending on how a particular person felt that particular week.

This sense of how the group's reception of her affected the speaker, links to the discussion below of witnessing.

The opportunity to respond to structure was crucial for the women who participated in my research, because having the freedom to create felt frightening. For someone whose whole life has been controlled, the option of free will might feel too threatening to the sense of self. It is therefore important to introduce elements of choice slowly and carefully. The abuse survivor has often forgotten how to trust her own impulses. As a child, her own sense of what seemed 'right' would have been undermined by the abuser.

- The structuring of space, with a carpeted area for talking and a linoleum area for action. This facilitated a movement into and out of anxiety-provoking material, possibly representing a movement between the child and adult selves. The partitioning of the studio seemed to provide a sense of security:

> Although there were people I knew and people I was getting to know and trusting I don't know, I felt safer sitting on a chair. I didn't feel so exposed. I suppose it was because of the reality of why I was here.

And yet the value was not just in being able to retreat:

> You do need movement, you do need to move out of the chair even if it's only to walk up, get in a circle and shake hands with people and say, I'm –, it's a nice day, how do you feel? Oh, pissed off, whatever. I think just to break…the tension.

This statement is corroborated by another woman, who described the move away from chairs as 'a lot of pressure off you', and by a third who felt that the move away from chairs could break up the intensity of verbal work. Some women felt singled out when gently encouraged by the therapists to contribute to verbal discussion. Discussion took place in the carpeted area, while seated in a circle of chairs. The sense of being singled out was exacerbated in smaller groups. The resultant sense of exposure may be reminiscent of the experience of abuse. This appears to be a function not just of being seen but of seeing. For example, one woman reflected: 'you were there and you had to face them and you had to look at them'. She seems to be saying here that the problem is one of facing something. She suggested that one solution to this difficulty might be for therapists to ask group members to choose a cushion and to sit where they wished, rather than be confined to a clearly demarcated circle of chairs.

However, another woman's experience was quite different. The 'check-in' at the beginning of each session contributed to her sense of support from the group. This arose precisely because she knew the focus would be on her if she needed it:

> if it was one person, that person would talk more and it felt better that like if I came in and I didn't feel so good that morning I would, it would be on me, the rest of the group would support me.

For one woman, the possibility of moving out of her chair and then back to it provided a sense that there were two rooms. This meant that the move back to a circle of chairs at the end of the session represented a move away from the therapists, and an 'easing down'.

There was one aspect of the arrangement of the room which was not entirely satisfactory: the circle of chairs on which each session began was, for two of the four groups studied, at the far end of the studio; this meant that each woman had to walk across an open space before reaching the chairs. Some of the women specifically mentioned this arrangement as unhelpful, particularly if they arrived late, as all eyes appeared to be watching while they walked across the space.

- A positive relationship with a key worker, who co-ordinated a package of care within the mental health service. This at best included prior disclosure work in individual therapy. The key worker ideally maintained regular contact and a sustaining relationship throughout the GAT-P.

One woman had had very little individual therapy prior to the GAT-P. She felt that the group setting provided less time for her than individual contact:

> I didn't feel safe enough...if one had a problem here within the group and it affected you, you had to either share it with the whole group really, or not share it. There was no one to share in a one to one...so I tended to take things home with me.

Nevertheless, this woman began to share more of herself with the group as she witnessed others doing so. Another woman who had had considerable individual therapy said that the group setting gave her a sense of increased attention, or perhaps a different kind of attention, than might be available in an individual therapy session.

The need for safety within the relationship between client and key worker was also discussed directly by certain research participants. One woman was facing the loss of her key worker, who was leaving her job around the time of the interview. This had apparently led to some worsening of symptoms. Another woman's trusting relationship with her key worker appeared to maximise her ability to take what she needed from the GAT-P. A third woman remarked that, while it was important that the group therapists treated her like an adult, it was also important that her key worker at times took caring control, as if she were a child.

One woman felt that the departure of a member of her group made her feel less secure. Following this event, she felt no improvement when she disclosed within the group. However, she did not actually feel worse, possibly because she was protected by the fact that her key worker was a trusted figure of long-standing. A second woman faced a particularly painful issue just before her holiday and at a time when her relationship with her key worker was still forming. This left her feeling worse because she was unable to fully integrate the experience.

Witnessing and being witnessed

Linked to the sense of safety was the concept of witnessing and being witnessed. The two phenomena of witnessing and being witnessed, though linked, may be entirely separate temporally in the survivor's recovery from abuse.

Witnessing appeared to occur both in relation to the CATs process, and independently as in group discussion. In both cases, benevolent witnessing appeared to provide an important 'mirror', facilitating change both in the witnessed and in the witness, rather as Jones (1996) proposes that the roles of actor and audience are both equally but differently powerful in drama-therapy practice. One woman describes the importance of this process:

> if you're strong enough that you can share, you can talk. You can relate to other people, you are not alone for that couple of hours or whatever. And there are people who can understand…and support…you… I mean, I've cried with other people in the group…to me it's important, that you didn't have to pretend. It was there for you.

The speaker seems to be implying a part of the recovery process which may be specific to the group context, namely the realisation that one is not alone in one's suffering, because others understand in a profound sense, through shared experience. This is what Yalom (1975) called 'universality'.

The experience of witnessing and being witnessed seems to link to the sense of being benevolently seen, heard and understood. Such a benevolent version of seeing and being seen directly contradicts the experience of abuse, in which the survivor will have been forced to witness that which she did not want to witness, and will have been seen intrusively rather than empathically.

One research participant hints that the awareness of no longer being alone might enable the individual to gain a new perspective:

> [What's helpful is]...being able to talk to people who understand, and that it's not a secret any more. The abuser then loses a hold on you, and that's such a release, it's like you're OK, it wasn't your fault you were the way you were.

This awareness is likely to increase the sense of safety, once the survivor decides to take the risk of being authentic in the group.

One woman said that the experience of hearing the stories of others helped her to feel she was not alone, despite the fact that children are abused in many different ways. For some survivors, the group therapy context provided the opportunity to witness others first, before being witnessed. The experience of witnessing others can be validating:

> It's not actually talking, but actually seeing people...when they've... talked about that on that day, how do they cope with it through a day? You know, can they shake it off and be totally happy you know, say sat around a dinner table? Do they actually go within themselves? Is it related between me and her? ... I can see those little daft things that we do between us, you know, and it sort of helps you without even talking about it.

When group members do have the opportunity to see how others have been affected by abuse, this can help the survivor to make sense of her own experience:

> Although every person's story was unique, finding that they had similar feelings and problems with their lives now, helped me a lot.

Certain themes emerge time and again in the women's statements about the experience of being in a group with other survivors. These include the sense of being understood; togetherness; no longer being alone; not being judged; and realising one is not mad. It was important that each woman was valued in the group for themselves. Contrary to Hazzard *et al.*'s (1993) findings, a heterogeneous group was seen by at least some women as useful:

> ...the way each person was made in some way to feel special, was very uplifting despite the very traumatic sessions; I felt we were all needed for ourselves and that each person gave a great deal to each session. Everybody gave a meaning and purpose to the group. Everybody genuinely cared for each other and knew what each other was feeling. The degree of abuse was not relevant, abuse was abuse.

Sometimes the witness by the group is active, for example when group members ask questions about a drawing made by one of them; at other times the witness is silent. This can be especially powerful and moving, as one woman describes:

> ...I can remember reading the poem and everybody was really, really quiet and I didn't need to say any more because the poem spoke for me ...it felt as though people understood. I think the silence from people was more helpful than if they'd said anything. It felt as though they understood what had really happened to me. It felt as though they accepted what had happened and it felt as though they were saying, without actually speaking, it's OK, we understand, we're with you. It felt as though they were with me in that...one or two just looked at each other and one looked as though she was going to cry...it was something very different than I'd experienced, because I'd never put myself in that situation where I ever opened up on more than a one to one... I think I felt the caring from them.

This led to a change in self-concept, allowing the individual to see herself as more acceptable to others. This transformation became possible through the witnessing of a creative form:

> ...the creative form speaks for you, but the reaction from the other people to the creative form comes back to you as a person.

The witnessing of others enables group members to work on issues at a distance. It can also lead to the ability to view experience from a new perspective. When one woman saw the photographs of other group members as children, she felt deep compassion for those children:

...so it made me think, it made me feel more it wasn't my fault. Because when I saw these photographs of other people and saw there was a little child I thought, that little child in that photograph can't defend itself. It's not capable of defending itself. It has no chance, it has to accept what comes, it can't counteract it, so it's not the child's fault, it's the adult's that did it. So then I identified that with myself and said I was a little child, so it wasn't my fault.

That the group therapists also act as witnesses is made clear by one woman's account of hearing one of the therapists (myself) read aloud to the group members a story she had written (see the section on guided imagery: the journey, pp.175–178). The story related a symbolic journey made by the group members from the beginning of the programme up to that point, near to the end of the programme:

As you're going along each week, you don't realise the progress you're making, and what sort of things you've done, even though you've done them, like you soon forget what you've done a few weeks before... I mean it took me a while when you was doing that 'journey' to realise it was us you was talking about! It did, honestly! ... And, so it was right helpful that it made you realise...how far you'd come forward from what you was.

Such witness involves the creativity of the therapists. Another example of this is in the use of a bill of rights (see p.142) constructed by one of the group therapists (again myself) from a 'brainstorm' by the group about their goals for therapy. The goals were typed up, with a copy to each group member, in the form of 'I have the right to...'. Of this, one woman said:

I've still got it, and if you are low, and you are down and pissed off...it's there to read and to put back into perspective, really...it reminds me of all the group, really.

The interesting point here is that the speaker remembers not the therapists' part in this co-created work, but that of the group as a whole, of which she herself was a part. This memory seemed to give her the strength to place her situation in perspective.

Group therapists do not only witness through their creativity. Equally important are the skills and attitudes adopted by any therapist:

I couldn't do it what you did, listen to six people and what they'd been through. And you was just so understanding, and you just helped us in every possible way. And you was as worried about us, and you was prepared to do something about it which I thought was very good.

Witnessing can also present a challenge:

> One of the therapists said you know like, if you're very sad you don't seem to be acting very sad right now ... which was totally new ... And I allowed myself to cry shortly afterwards which I don't very often ... It's had the permanent effect of a realisation that for example yesterday I was in a pretty bad predicament. I was very, very upset and I needed an outlet to cry, but in general life there was no room for it ... I mean I knew I was angry yesterday because I was really sad.

One woman explains how being witnessed by the other group members can assist survivors to see the abuse differently from the way they did as a child (in her case linked to her religious and cultural heritage):

> Because you're telling somebody and they actually believe you. 'Cos when you're a small child, a ____ [religious] child, it's a very big thing to be doing things like that, and to actually admit it you're admitting it to God as well. You know, that you are not being the guilty one, you didn't do it, you know. But you think God thinks oh well, she's letting him do this that and the other. Because you're child-like.

I shall now discuss each task in the recovery process in turn.

Striving: struggling to survive, burial and the dilemma of embodiment

Introduction to striving

The women who participated in my research study voluntarily spoke of their struggle, which began long before the GAT-P and continued throughout it, becoming more acute at various stages. They spoke about the following, most of which are well documented in the general literature on CSA and its sequelae (see Chapter 1), and which can be viewed as attempts to survive:

- a history of parasuicide and self-harming: there was some evidence that rates of self-harming reduced after the programme, which supports den Herder and Redner's (1991) suggestion that self-harming rates may offer one way to evaluate therapeutic programmes

- difficulties in attending group meetings, with a tendency to use medication to cope with pre-session anxiety, particularly early in the programme
- difficulties in verbalisation in group sessions and elsewhere
- difficulties with writing, whether connected to literacy difficulties or not
- a vulnerability to life events (e.g. child care issues, or unplanned contact with the abuser), resulting in a worsening of symptoms
- a sense of two selves battling against each other
- 'flashbacks', in which the abuse is relived in the present, as if it is happening now
- a tendency to misinterpret what others say, taking this as criticism
- self-blame for the abuse
- burial of memories
- feeling 'flat', and being detached from feelings, even when recalling and relating details of the abuse
- a sense that the 'good' feelings are hidden along with the 'bad' feelings, like weeds choking flowers
- a sense that the abuser is contained inside one's own body
- substance misuse
- eating disorders
- avoidance of sex, or promiscuity without any real intimacy
- out-of-body experiences
- psychosomatic disorders, including irritable bowel syndrome, nausea, dizziness and headaches: one woman had had a pain in her foot for some time, which disappeared following some cathartic work that involved kicking a dummy around the room
- avoidance of looking in mirrors
- the need to bath after each session, or avoidance of bathing
- difficulties in engaging in physical activities both within and outside of the programme.

Struggling to survive

In the early stages of recovery, the survivor of sexual abuse is literally struggling to survive. For some of the women in this study, this meant a history of parasuicide and many were actively self-harming (see the dilemma of embodiment) before their GAT-P started. Indeed, for some research participants this was still a risk following the GAT-P. For example, one woman said:

> I feel like I could just top myself quite easily, and then as the strong bit grows, it's either one or the other of the two. And I can't remember it afterwards...well I can't believe that I really felt that way. I'll do something ridiculous, I'll cut myself or something, and I think, why did I do that? Crazy.

For most of the research participants, the recovery process itself was seen as a struggle. Some women acknowledged that although they had found the programme beneficial they had not wanted to attend the group meetings, finding these so stressful that they wanted to withdraw rather than socialise after sessions. Some women spoke of physical responses including nausea either prior to or after each session, particularly early in the programme (see the dilemma of embodiment).

Several women had difficulty in speaking openly about themselves, and one woman observed that in her group the members had avoided talking about the abuse:

> we were all waiting for somebody else to do it, I think. You know, one part of you wants to get on with it, but that 'no, I want to run away from it' is also there.

Here, the speaker seems to be referring to the group members' difficulties in facing the abuse. One research participant found it very upsetting to hear other women's accounts of their abuse. This point is in contrast to the value of witnessing and being witnessed described earlier. Several of the women who experienced difficulties in talking in the group found that the creative activities provided a more accessible alternative. However, writing tasks presented problems for some women who had literacy difficulties or for whom writing may have also been linked with the process of facing the reality of the abuse. One woman, for example, said:

> it was a nightmare having to write it down. I completely ignored [one of the group therapists] when she was talking. I really flipped.

The struggle faced by survivors often includes a struggle to relate to others. This can manifest itself in avoidance of either forming close relationships within the group; attending the last session; or recontacting other group members after the GAT-P, for fear of rejection.

Some women described a worsening of their symptoms following disclosure. This happened if disclosure occurred at a stage in their recovery when they did not feel sufficiently safe. Others described difficulties in maintaining improvements following the GAT-P, due to life events beyond their control. One woman described her concerns about the need to keep up the momentum of recovery:

> it's churned things up, and loosened things to the state where, if I don't do anything any further, it's all going to start to settle back and you know, maybe in the end it won't make a big enough improvement.

Several of the women said that they felt twenty weeks to be insufficient to guarantee a permanent recovery. One woman indicated that her longest held beliefs about herself and the world easily returned. These beliefs included a sense of guilt and self-blame about the abuse. She concluded that she needed longer in therapy:

> I think it's just with the longer term issues that…have started creeping back up on me. Whereas I suppose it's a bit like getting over a cold, I think. You know, you come off your remedy too soon and then things start creeping back later on.

One woman's perception, when she began self-harming again following a particularly stressful life event, was that she was 'going round in circles' rather than recovering. It is possible that in fact she was perceiving a function of the spirallic nature of the recovery process proposed here. As with the climbing of a spiral staircase, the view of a certain point will be similar with each turn, but not precisely the same.

Some gains were dependent on the situation. For example, a woman might assert herself if something seemed to threaten her children's safety or well-being, but still be unable to believe that she herself was worth defending in this way. One woman spoke of her bitterness that she had been made to suffer. She described the abuse as 'a cancer, spreading through the whole of my life', which was exacerbated by the stigma of having been a psychiatric patient.

One research participant reflected that the recovery process cannot be effected simply by deciding to change:

I've talked it through and said what I think I want to feel, but it's not actually worked out in practice. Words are fine. I can say yes, I feel great, yes this will happen, oh yes, that doesn't bother me. It's very easy to say that, but putting it into practice is not always the same.

Many of the statements made by research participants illustrate the struggling survivor's sense that much of the process is internal, experienced as a battle between two parts of the self, which can be very tiring. Some women described the two sides as like child and adult selves:

There's this adult bit of me saying this is fine, you're not going to bother when you see him in the street 'cos he's a big bully and he's not going to hurt you and you're grown up now, you're not a little girl. When he's there, all that like goes out of the window and I'm sort of this trembling mass that wants to run off or run up my mum's coat which is what I really did when he was there, just wanted to hide behind her. So I just can't get the two together.

Some women found that their 'inner child' was now more real following the GAT-P, experienced more in the present than in the past, though most appear to have passed through this stage during the programme and eventually developed a more balanced and integrated sense of self. Associated with the battle between the 'child self' and the 'adult self' was the survivor's disbelief in her own innocence. Most of the research participants referred to having blamed themselves for the abuse prior to the GAT-P, although several of them had shifted this view following the programme, to attributing blame for the abuse at least to some extent to the abuser. The tendency to blame oneself can be understood within the context of the 'child self' dominating in the early stages of recovery. For the abused child, it is much easier to accept blame than to believe that the trusted adult is to blame, especially when the abuser is reinforcing this view (Herman 1992).

The resolution of the experience of abuse was itself seen as a struggle by some of the research participants. Some women said that the abuse by one perpetrator had been resolved, but not that perpetrated by a second adult. Others reported that the abuser, though dead, was still 'alive' inside the survivor's head. For some women, confrontation with one or other parent remained a desired outcome, but was too terrifying a prospect to be attempted without a very great sense of safety.

For some women, there was a definite ambivalence about recovery. One woman described this in terms of difficulties in reclaiming control after feeling out of control all her life. Another woman expressed her struggle as on the one hand feeling that she ought to feel completely clear of the memory of the abuse, and on the other hand:

> maybe that's nonsense, we should be more practical, maybe I'll have this memory, that I can look at like a scar.

This comment seems to allude to the possibility of laying the abuse to rest.

Despite in some cases wanting a male partner, most women found themselves still afraid of men at the end of the GAT-P, a fear which often prevented medical examination by a male doctor.

One woman's words sum up the desperate struggle of the survivor: 'I will survive... I will survive, but it's so hard.' But she also suggests that through such struggling may come some reward:

> But it's frightening; the mind's a very strange thing. But I'll conquer it and put a flag on the mountain.

Burial

Concurrent with the struggle to survive is the process of burial, which is a coping mechanism acquired during childhood in response to the abuse, and continued in adulthood. This process as I am using the term here refers to the burial of feelings and sometimes of memories, and is linked to the condition often described as 'dissociation' and also to Herman's (1992) category of 'numbing'. I am using the word 'burial' here in preference to the word dissociation for two reasons: first, because the word 'dissociation' implies some distance, whereas the aim of the survivor may be to gain some distance from the experience of abuse but the result is often quite different; second, dissociation is a word defined by the medical profession and yet the word burial, or the concept of burial, was the one used consistently by my research participants and is therefore likely to more authentically reflect their experience. In cases of clinical dissociation as defined by DSM-IV (American Psychiatric Association 1994) the survivor may have out-of-body experiences, for example (depersonalisation). However, once consciousness is realigned with the physical self there is a sense in which the whole experience of abuse is internalised and embodied in the way described below. The phenomenon of burial is thus intrinsically linked to the dilemma of embodiment. Once the recovery process begins and memories become unearthed the burial process is shown for what it is, rather than a true distancing from the abuse. One woman's comments show her puzzlement that she could have buried something so crucial at one stage, since her memories now were vivid:

> when something has been buried for thirty odd years, that takes some getting used to. And having sat in groups and saying thank God that never happened to me – and I've done that here, three years ago. There was a woman who'd been sexually abused in a group I was in, and I said thank God it didn't happen to me…that's what I find hard to accept, how can something be so deep within your mind?

The ambivalence experienced by some survivors concerning gaps in memory is eloquently expressed by one woman:

> I find it difficult, the bits that I can't remember. On the other hand, there are times when I don't want to remember, but there are times when I find it difficult; it's like an incomplete picture with missing pieces.

Another woman spoke of her initial inclination being to hide her feelings, to the extent that when she had spoken of the abuser for the first time she had felt nothing and 'just sort of went flat'. The location of the hidden material inside the survivor, and the importance of this process in struggling to survive is evident in her statement that:

> I think if you can be very detached about it and just say, these are the facts of what happened, and not have any feelings about it, that almost is an easier thing. But to say well it hurt me, it's damaged me, and this is what it's done – it's like really taking all the barriers down, that… It's like opening a gate, a door, you'll let people see in, but you want to know that door is still there so you can pull it back again.

However, she also recognised that:

> it's not just the bad things that are closed up inside you, it's all the good qualities that could have developed. And they can't, they're choking. You know, it's like weeds choking the flowers, you've got to get rid of them and pull enough up to let them grow.

This woman's comments suggest that there is a part of the self which has been stifled by the experience of abuse, and which needs nurturing in order to develop.

Another woman found that after the GAT-P had ended she began to bury the abuse again, but not to forget. Her statement suggests that there has been some unearthing, and is reminiscent of those above which refer to two sides battling:

because I haven't seen you for this length of time, I think, well I'll just bury it again. And then I think, no I'm not. It's out now.

The expressed need for a flexible number of sessions was linked by one woman to 'a lifetime of hiding away from these things'. She later indicated that the experience of abuse was internalised, by saying 'for all these years I've kept it down'. Another woman argued for longer sessions (we responded to this by increasing the length from one and a half to two hours in the following GAT-P), as she could 'bury it within an hour and a half' which resulted in her failing to say what she needed to say. This particular woman felt that if the GAT-P had included for example a residential element, she may have felt more able to open up.

The results from the use of a self-assessment proforma (see p.132) used for the last two groups indicated that anger, painful feelings, joy, memories of the abuse and a sense of self were all at times buried by survivors, particularly in the early stages of recovery. This would mean in practice that anger was often turned inwards on the self, sometimes through the use of both legal and illegal substances to assist in the burial, and often through self-injury (see the dilemma of embodiment).

Recovery of access to feelings carries some risk with it, as one woman described:

> I used to be able to switch off to any person. I can't now. I can't switch my feelings off, either. And I don't think it's very good, that. I'd rather be able to switch off.

It should be noted that this woman's experience was atypical, however. On the whole, the recovery of feelings was seen as a positive process. Most women felt they could have some control of this, provided that the pace had not been rushed by their own sense of urgency. For example, one woman saw the need to move away from burial in order to progress in her recovery. She could still hide herself when talking, but was less likely to do so when using creative media:

> when I was verbalising it wasn't the real me that was coming through. It was only the part that I wanted to come through that came through in the words, the parts that I felt were acceptable and that I thought weren't going to cause me to be upset or cause anybody else to have any problems with it. So if I verbalised very occasionally in the group, it was only perhaps to help somebody else out, or if I was directed with a question. But it wasn't in any great depth.

The dilemma of embodiment

Herman (1992) has already written at some length concerning the tendency towards either numbing of bodily sensations and/or intrusive thoughts and imagery (see Chapter 1). I have also written about what I see as 'the dilemma of embodiment' for survivors of CSA (Meekums 1995). The dilemma is that there is a need to reclaim and re-inhabit one's body, yet to do so may be retraumatising since this is the site of intrusions which threatened one's very sense of self, and potentially one's existence. Simonds (1994) suggests that the route whereby body and mind are reconnected may be a long and indirect one, depending on the severity of 'dissociative' defences.

The act of burial discussed above implies paradoxically a cutting off from feelings and from the body, and yet burial has reference to the body as a container of feelings and memories. This was evidenced by one or more of the following: high degrees of somatisation; acts of self-harming; denial of body sensations; bingeing and vomiting; and problems in experiencing sexual feeling.

The importance of beginning to address this dilemma is made clear in one woman's statement:

> it's in here, it's still here. I suppose in a way it's still festering, but it's not getting inflamed because I'm not – I'm trying not to let it, let's put it that way. Whereas before to me it was like a big septic sore, and everything needed to come out.

This woman clearly felt that something was contained within her (she pointed to her body), which needed to come out, alluding to the process of unearthing. Her metaphoric language may indicate a need both to communicate something very complex and to refer to it obliquely.

Another woman's description of her self-injury is indicative of just one rationale used by survivors to explain this type of behaviour. She explained what happened when she became angry with her husband for some reason:

> I would reach a point where I was going to go too far, and I was aware of it that much, and so would then go up and do something to myself... I would never do it in front of him, I would have to go away, be on my own, do something like that, and then come down and have a reasonable discussion with him. It wasn't something that I'd do to say you've made me feel this bad, therefore I'm going to do this. It wasn't like that. It sort of focused everything again, by doing it. I hate to say it, but it still does.

And regarding her eating disorder:

> if I do it in anger, then I will eat purposely foods that I know I hate. I won't eat anything I like.

One woman felt physically sick on the mornings prior to group meetings for the first ten to twelve weeks, that is for over half of the programme. Another, suffering from irritable bowel syndrome, would need Valium before each of the first four sessions. A third felt tense before each session, her head would seem to tighten, and she would become forgetful. She would also experience pains in her stomach and back, and have diarrhoea. A fourth said that she tended to feel a tightness in her chest when she thought about the abuse. One woman indicated that the degree of her symptomatology was evident by how she felt physically; when unwell she would feel dizzy and tired. The thought of one of the abusers continued to make her feel nauseous as an adult, as it had when she was a child. She describes a particularly powerful session in the GAT-P which clearly illustrates the process of embodiment:

> I had a terrible pain in my foot from, oh for about three month during that group until the end, and it was really bad. And if I stayed up late and I'd have got really tired, I'd be awake all night because the pain would go right up my leg. In the end I asked my doctor to look at it because I thought maybe there was something physically wrong. It wasn't. But was it in the second or third from last that we did, when we had the figure on the floor and I jumped on it, stamped on it? I wondered, I thought well my foot might give way, it's hurting that much. And it didn't. A week later, the pain had gone completely. It started to go from then.

Some women felt the need to wash and change after each session:

> I just had to get home, and get my clothes off and get in the bath and cry, and try to cry it out of my system.

In contrast, other women would avoid bathing because they felt ashamed of their bodies.

The difficulties in making use of dance movement therapy structures in the early stages of recovery are highlighted by one woman:

> when you're shaking a cloth around with a ball on it you think, well what's the purpose of this? And I felt negative, and I felt angry. I thought: What is this going to achieve? What is this going to solve?

This woman admitted at her interview that her anger had arisen because the activity had reminded her of her own experience. As a child, she had felt like the ball that was being tossed around. Her bewilderment concerning the usefulness of movement in therapy was echoed by a second woman in a later GAT-P, despite careful attempts to explain and illustrate DMT at assessment. Another woman did not like any of the activities that required one-to-one contact of any sort. Group participants were given free choice about the degree of contact; for example, pair dances could be carried out with fingertips touching, or with a prop between them such as a pair of garden canes.

One woman had expected to enjoy the dance movement and drama-based activities, as she had been dancing for years. She was surprised to find herself 'in a shell' and even quite angry. She concluded that it had something to do with the context. DMT suggested a different way of using dance from the 'time out' she had experienced previously when dancing:

> Maybe when the dance was put in the therapy for me it didn't feel quite comfortable, because it was a part of something that wasn't comfortable anyway.

The positive experiences of DMT described by some of the other research participants are in contrast to the views of these women. One research participant, for example, had previously experienced touch as difficult. However, when she danced with a partner in fingertip contact, it felt not only non-threatening but pleasurable, which she attributed at least in part to the use of rhythm.

It was at a group meeting during which preliminary findings of the research were discussed, that further clarification of the role of dance movement-based activities was sought. In general, those performed in a circle to set steps were perceived as connecting the individual to the group. They were experienced as less threatening than expressive movement. The problem with expressive movement was that it might use the space more freely, or allow for a focus on one individual, leading to a feeling of being exposed. As children, these women had felt watched by the abuser. The abuse was physical in the sense that it occurred through their bodies, so that any physical experience had the potential to bring back painful memories. Timing was crucial in introducing the more expressive elements of movement and dance. This clearly links to the need for the establishment of safety. In addition to the issue of safety, one woman said that the level of cutting off from body sensations which she experienced made it difficult to know how her own body wanted to move. This led to a feeling of not being good enough as a person, which in itself was associated with the experience of abuse. On the other hand, some of the more structured dances made some women feel powerful. The progression from very structured movement towards freer expression facilitated a process of desensitisation to anxiety provoking associations. The role of circle dance is described by one woman:

> I think it was really good because everybody did it and it was done fairly early on in the group...it brought the group together as a whole and it made that physical contact with people... You are prepared to really reach out to other people within the group. If someone's upset, that you are prepared to give them a hug and say, look I really care. And I think it was the start of that really... And it was a very simple dance so nobody was struggling with it... I felt it really broke the ice, that.

Although several of the group participants were in a sexual partnership (eight out of fourteen to my knowledge), of these, five disclosed either during interview or during other contacts with myself (for example during the therapy or assessment process) that they experienced some difficulties with sex. As many as six of the fourteen research participants appeared to be celibate. One woman described how television items concerning abuse had a negative effect on her sex life: 'it totally knocks me sick, sex-wise'. She rather poignantly remarked: 'I don't feel I'll ever understand what true or nice sex is', and although she knew she should not see her body as dirty, she did. Some women found that the experience of pregnancy, childbirth or lactation had a negative effect both on their sex-life and on their recovery from CSA trauma.

While Simonds (1994) is emphatic that the body itself must be a major topic in therapy at some point due to the impact of sexual trauma on the body, the results of my own research would point to the need for caution in addressing the issue. As Sanderson (1995), writing from a clinical perspective, states: 'Experiential techniques which focus on the body are often the most distressing and emotionally arousing of all the experiential/exploratory techniques' (p.149). She suggests that these techniques, which might include body awareness techniques, massage, 'rolfing' (deep tissue massage) and 'primal scream therapy', should be used only after the survivor has become desensitised through considerable exploration of the abuse; there has been some resolution of the trauma; and she has learned breathing and desensitisation techniques which enable her to maintain a relatively stable level of arousal. However, Sanderson does suggest that dance and movement may be useful for the survivor in enhancing awareness of the body, increasing its fluidity, developing the capacity for pleasure from the body, and alleviating dissociation. She also suggests that breathing and grounding exercises (often used by dance movement therapists and described by Simonds 1994) can increase the survivor's sense of personal power and control.

Incubation: letting go into the art form resulting in unearthing, facing the reality and speaking the unspeakable

Introduction to incubation

Engagement with the art form appears simultaneously to facilitate:

- the unearthing of material including memories, images and feelings which have been previously located at least partially in the unconscious or buried in some way; this is accompanied by a sense of shock or surprise

- confrontation or facing the reality of what was previously (at least in part) buried or denied: confrontation occurs through the production of an image or feelings which can be faced as acknowledged reality

- a sense that the art form speaks that reality for the individual, and possibly for the group.

The act of letting go into the art form as part of a therapeutic intervention is obviously specific to the arts therapies context. It is quite possible that there are parallels in other therapeutic approaches. Further research would be needed to establish this.

It is impossible at this stage to separate temporally the three aspects of letting go into the art form which are outlined above. However, they are three distinct functions and therefore will be addressed here in turn.

Unearthing

One of the research participants' references to unearthing give some clues about its link to the creative process as it has been described elsewhere (see, e.g. Boden 1990; Meekums 1993), in that it is most likely to occur when there is a letting go of conscious control:

> I've found that things come back to me, either when I'm asleep, dreaming, or just before you go to sleep, or when you're just relaxed and

your mind's gone off things completely, you're sort of switched off from all that. And then you suddenly find things just come back to you.

This statement places the phenomenon of unearthing within the creative process (see Chapter 2), but implies that it is not unique to the arts therapies context. Another woman's account throws more light on the significance of unearthing within the context of arts therapies modalities:

> I felt it was coming from within. I wasn't thinking, 'oh I'm going to draw a painting of myself now'. I didn't set off with an idea I'm going to draw a picture of trees. I got the piece of paper and something from within me set the painting and I just drew…if I dance, the dancing comes from within. I don't say I'm going to do this step or that step… So I think it's a means of getting in touch with your inner self and the part that's really you.

Unearthing thus seems to be associated with the use of arts modalities within an unstructured or semi-structured form. So, for example, a scripted piece of drama or a choreographed dance would be less likely to evoke strong personal imagery than an improvisation. However, structured art forms as we have seen may contribute to some self-understanding when evaluated. They may also assist in the containment of feeling and in the establishment of a sense of safety. Unearthing thus seems to be a way of accessing an authentic, previously hidden or buried self:

> I have become aware of how much I am releasing with the movement and the rhythm and the contact with a part of me, really, which has been kept in a sort of…a box, for so many years.

It also seems to imply a bridging between the present and some aspect of the past:

> I've loved the dance, I've loved the movement…which in a way has triggered things like when I was a youngster… And there was just the memory of that enjoyment, which was really a sort of bridge back to what was good in my childhood.

This last statement is interesting, in that it supports the claim made by Simonds (1994) that art and movement 'can serve as a bridge between the unspoken and the spoken, between the unknown and the known, between the unconscious and the conscious' (p.1).

This is not a new idea; the eminent psychiatrist and psychoanalyst, Winnicott (1971), wrote at some length concerning the function of creative approaches to psychotherapy in bridging this gap. As discussed briefly in Chapter 2, he proposed that creative activities take place in what he termed the notional 'potential space' (p.126) between mother and infant, which later becomes a potential space between the individual and the environment (p.118).

Unearthing is a delicate process that can be perceived as a surprise or shock. One woman indicated that at times she felt that unearthing happened against her conscious will, referring to a sense of something being 'pulled from you'. Another research participant referred to the abuse as:

> stored inside us like a time bomb... And it's really...how you get it out without hurting yourself, without killing yourself through getting it out.

Notwithstanding this caution, she went on to say:

> But it's the getting it out – and once you get a bit of it out and you work it through over and over again the pain goes less and less from it, 'til at the end you think no, I don't want to talk through that again.

Not all that is unearthed feels comfortable or good:

> I don't think I realised quite how I felt about anything before. The group has put me more in touch with what I feel generally, so that includes the bad things and the good things...everything I feel is just much more acute now.

This can feel devastating for the survivor who has coped by dissociating from body and feelings, but one woman explained why the process of unearthing is important:

> the more you dig away at those things and get them out of you...the less control they have over you.

Unearthing can reveal more fodder for therapy:

> I think that to have cleared out...my cupboard once, I think I find there's more there in the way of discomfort.

The process of raising to consciousness those issues which were previously 'buried' appears from my research to have been an important, though not necessarily the most important, aspect of the recovery process. As discussed in Chapter 1, Berry (1997) would argue against its importance. It is worth noting that the CSA of which Berry writes does not necessarily fall into the category of repeated trauma, which may be enforced through threats to the life of the victim or to others whom she loves. As we have seen, Herman

(1992) suggests that this repeated trauma might lead to what she calls 'complex post-traumatic stress disorder'. It is possible, if Herman's analysis is correct, that such repeated trauma, perpetrated in childhood, has a profound effect on the developing sense of self. A single incident from which the victim is enabled to recover through a loving, supportive and believing family may be traumatic, but would not injure the developing ego in quite the same way. All of the women participating in my study apparently had histories of repeated trauma of the type which is likely, according to Herman (1992), to lead to 'complex post-traumatic stress disorder'. It remains a matter for future research to more firmly establish, possibly via comparison groups, whether or not the recovery of memories in this context is an essential condition in the process of recovery. It seems likely that as Jones (1991) suggests, it is the relevant account (as defined by the survivor herself) which needs to be narrated by the survivor in therapy. This may not necessarily be the whole account of the abuse.

The debate concerning FMS, discussed in Chapters 1 and 2, is also relevant here. Group therapists must be careful not to suggest that new memories can or should be elicited. The potentially powerful role of CATs in generating images from the unconscious must be viewed with caution. Kane's (1989) distinction (discussed in Chapter 1) between 'fantastica', which lack the balance of sensation and the mediation of thinking and feeling functions, and true imagination, could have clinical value.

In this sense, the unearthing of images may be one way in which the CATs link to a spiritual or 'shamanic' journey (see Chapter 2), similar to a journey into the depths of the unconscious. Alternatively, the whole 'journey' of recovery can be seen as a heroine's quest for the self, via the metaphoric slaying and laying to rest of the demon of abuse. It is interesting to note, that there were few if any overt references to spiritual phenomena by research participants, although it could be argued that they are implicit in such phrases as 'laying to rest'. It may be, that the experience of abuse robs the individual of their 'spirit', and that it is the embodied 'spirit' which must be reclaimed and assert itself. Further research concerning the spiritual aspects of recovery is needed, to throw light on this topic.

Facing the reality

Facing the reality appears to be associated with a growing sense of things becoming more real, and links directly to the next stage of the process, gaining a new perspective. One research participant discovered that when she made a drawing of the room in which she was repeatedly abused:

> it made me admit how old I actually was when it happened...it made me admit that it did happen to me.

Facing the reality of the abuse is inevitably a painful process, in itself a part of the struggle of each survivor:

> it was having to face reality for that allotted time each week, you know, that you couldn't, well, if you were sensible you didn't run away from it. And that was very hard, sticking with it. That really was hard.

Despite this difficulty, several women spoke of the necessity of 'hitting the abuse head on', and that when they did so this was a 'big step forward'.

The conflict and struggle inherent in facing painful issues is illustrated by the following account. The woman is referring to her difficulties in recording details of the abuse on paper, during one of the GAT-P sessions:

> There's a conflict there. It was helpful that it brought me to face my mother properly, although it really hurt. And the other way, well I don't think it would have made me face things if I hadn't have done it. I had to do it...it happened and you've got to write it down, it happened. Sometimes you think, how could anybody have done that to you...there was obviously tears, and the smashing things up, and I didn't speak for days and I cried a lot, then it just seemed to pass. It was really hard. I told myself my mother did love me because I couldn't cope with that she didn't love me, you see... [I now] realise she's a human being, I think, and human beings do wrong sometimes; we can't all be perfect, no matter how you strive to be.

This statement deals with the woman's experience of facing the fact that not nly was she sexually abused, but also her mother physically abused her. The ᵀmath of facing this fact was initially that she felt worse but this feeling ᵗ after some time and eventually she saw both herself and her mother ew perspective.

Speaking the unspeakable

Herman (1992) presents some research evidence for the importance of telling the narrative of the abuse, as discussed in Chapter 1. However, I refer in this section not simply to verbal expression but to a much wider range of human expression. The experience of 'speaking' and being heard links very closely to the vector catalyst of witnessing and being witnessed. Above all, the witness must not judge the survivor, nor take over feeling for the survivor.

The importance of speaking out is highlighted by the following woman's regret that she had not been able to disclose details of her abuse:

> I just felt that if I'd been able to say out loud, you know, to speak it out, because it's in your mind, I feel it would have made a difference.

Several women remarked that 'words are not enough'. The arts modalities appear to have provided a valuable alternative to using words in the usual way. This helped, both in understanding the contributions of others and in finding ways to say something they could not previously express:

> It just felt really great to know that... I could draw that image of me being that little child and I wanted help.

While facing the reality is often associated with painful feelings, speaking through the art form appears to provide a container or distancer for these feelings:

> I was sort of talking about the drawing. It was easier because I had something there to hold up. It was almost like having a mask in front of me, it was almost like something with me, as if I was hiding behind a mask really and it was the painting that was speaking... It's not me speaking it's the dance speaking. It's not me speaking it's the drama speaking. That's how it became really. The other thing took over.

By using the art form to speak for her, one woman was able to develop a capacity for using her voice in the group, an activity that had previously felt too confronting. She illustrated this point with reference to a poem that she had created about what happened to her as a little girl. She said that it was as if the child inside her was writing. When she later read the poem aloud to the group:

> I was using my voice, I was verbalising. It was a form of verbalisation, which I found very difficult in the group. I didn't want to verbalise my feelings, I didn't want to sit in a circle and tell people what was going on inside me. And yet the poem was telling people about my past, it was

telling them about when I was [young], which I wouldn't have – I wouldn't have sat here and spoken about when I was [young]... And yet with the poem I had to speak it. So it was using my voice to speak, which was the first time I'd done it in the group, the first time I'd really said anything about my life in a verbal form.

The speaker made the distinction between this kind of communication, which is authentic, comes from within and connects to feelings 'deep down inside' and the kind of verbalisation she could manage relatively easily, which came from her intellect but was unconnected to this source.

One woman discovered that the arts provided something which she found more beneficial than talking; she described the activities as loosening up her tight head and helping her to 'bring it out', which resulted in a kind of release. This sense of relief or release was echoed by others. One woman spoke of free movement providing an opportunity to 'let our bodies go and just relax and calm down', while another woman found relief in engaging cathartically with a larger-than-life dummy:

> it's the one of beating that image around the room. I found that so thera-
> peutic, and I spent the next two or three weeks just enjoying the memory
> of doing it. And it wasn't in any way vindictive, or it just seemed right,
> you know. It just seemed as if there was all this energy that had built up
> and it needed that channel to be released and then I could move on.

She went on to say that since she had released her anger in the group she no longer wasted her energy by feeling 'stuck' in her anger with the abuser.

There is an implication in the statements about speaking through the arts therapies activities of something new and fresh, connecting with something past:

> I had never written it down before. I'd never actually explained and
> vocalised to anybody in detail what had happened, ...using words for
> the parts of the anatomy that I had never done before, in relation to
> myself.

One woman found that the arts activities provided a way of calming her feelings when some of the verbal work had been addressing painful areas:

> after we'd done some work here that was a little bit traumatic, ...we were
> able to go over there and stick a paint brush through a piece of paper and
> splodge paint everywhere. And it had a sort of calming effect, I found.
> Same with free movement; that gave me a sense of relief, jumping round

like you do when you're a kid. You don't tend to do it when you're older, but to be able to just run round and act stupid for five minutes was really, really good. Maybe I should do that a bit more.

However, not everyone finds the arts to be the best media for expression. One research participant found the CATs activities very difficult, which may in part have been due to her belief that she was not artistic. For her, group discussion was a more accessible vehicle for expression than creative activities. When self-trust is damaged (Herman 1992) to the extent that the survivor is unable to access creative modalities, words (though difficult) may provide the only route. Winnicott (1971, p.118) suggests that the 'potential space' in which play and other creative acts can occur becomes accessible only if the infant's early relationship with the mother and the environment is dependable. When the mother and the environment are dependable, the infant is able to 'introject' a sense of trust. Another important aspect of Winnicott's (1971) theory is his suggestion that early play experiences are significant in building the infant's sense of self. Winnicott's 'ego' is not a body ego in the sense of being related to body function, but is founded on body experiences (p.118) which arise out of the relationship with the caregiver. Winnicott does not directly address the context of CSA. However, his theory is consistent with the view that CSA could endanger a sense of self. It is also consistent with the suggestion that CSA damages both trust in one's own instincts and trust in the actions of others. One other possible explanation for the difficulties experienced by some research participants in using creative media is the idea that creative expression reveals the innermost thoughts and feelings of the individual. When that individual has learned to survive by hiding the self in any number of ways, such revelation could be experienced as threatening. For those who preferred creative activities to ver-balisation, however, it was a relief not to have to put into words their complex experiences and feelings. Some were surprised both at what they had created, and at how relevant this was to their situation. It should be remembered here, that the CATs are not just a group of non-verbal techniques. Verbalisation, while not the sole focus of therapy, is integral to most CATs practice, and is frequently stimulated by the use of a creative structure. However, a consider-ation of the individual's ability to make use of creative tools is important in assessment. This point is given due consideration in Chapter 4.

The research itself appears to have provided a means of speaking out for most of the women who volunteered. In discussing her reasons for volunteer-ing, one woman declared:

> sometimes I feel like standing up and saying to people…and I get angry, but it's a different anger that I really want to get across to people the importance. They've no idea unless they've been there, and how can they?

For most of these women, the opportunity to speak out also had an altruistic component:

> I can see that this is an opportunity for me to give what knowledge I've got and my experiences, to be used.

> Nothing is ever being done about it because nobody knows about it. I feel as if it's probably my little way of doing something about it… I think that should be your criteria really, because you feel that nobody's been there for you.

> To me it's kept quiet too much, isn't it? I mean, I know you read things now and again about it, but it's not as often as, you know, some things. It's like – I think if there was something there that you could read, and somebody could understand into, 'cos I mean you know yourself if you talk to people it's still sort of taboo, in a way. And with research and sort of more understanding into it, then maybe it wouldn't be as taboo.

> I think for loads of people my sort of age there wasn't much help available when we were being abused, and people are a bit more aware of it now. I think by being part of the research, I'd like to think that people will learn the sort of things they're likely to – you know what I mean – the effects of it on people.

The need to speak or express oneself in some way and be 'heard' (witnessed) appears in many ways to be central to the survivor's therapy, since abuse is so often marked by secrecy, disbelief and even judgements on the victim. This learned silence and secrecy appears to be reinforced by the refusal of society, at times, to listen. The repression of the truth of CSA is evident historically (Masson 1992; Olafson et al. 1993). It has also come to light that when the zealousness of professionals in identifying CSA has been questioned, resulting in public outcry and official investigations, children have been returned to abusive homes despite their attempts to seek help (Gerrard 1997). Gerrard warns: 'Even today, we can easily ignore the signs written on children's bodies and encoded in their behaviour' (p.3), while Simonds (1994) urges therapists to become (symbolically) the caring parents who notice these clues.

Illumination: gaining a new perspective

The experience of letting go into the art form with benevolent witnesses, or witnessing others, eventually leads to cognitive shifts. Very often, these shifts appear to be associated with a shift in self-perception from child to adult and from victim to assertive survivor. This shift enables a new integration of child and adult selves. The metaphor of a shift in position is evident in the following woman's description of her position relative to her mother:

> I always stand there in the background...behind my mum. That's my usual position, behind my mum. It always has been, the whole of my life. And my mum's the one that gives it out and everything...I still tend to sort of stand behind, I still do it but I know that if I want to stand there in front, I can do it if I want to.

The speaker seems to be implying a greater level of assertion, which was reported by several of the research participants:

> I can express myself ... I couldn't do it when I was a child when I was being hurt. I couldn't even do it in my bloody marriage, four years ago ... nobody's going to cry me down and tell me to shut up or smack me across the face because I've opened my mouth, you know.

One woman remembered the psychodramatic representation of a swimming pool (see p.152) in reclaiming her outgoing nature:

> when we did the 'swimming pool' I was quite impressed with myself. I discovered how outgoing and adventurous I was. Because I forget that I am quite capable... I was on the diving board and...that made me feel quite positive, you know. I mean, as a child I never went swimming so, I have got over some aspects, you know? But I found that just – it helped me recognise myself a little bit.

The shift in perspective seems to provide greater clarity, which may manifest as a greater awareness of what is often referred to as the 'inner child':

> I feel like I know me better, you know, inside... I sort of understand more about that little girl inside, that I never understood before. I understood the hurt, but I didn't understand what was going on.

This ability to empathise with the 'inner child' can lead to an awareness that the little girl who was abused was not to blame. The change is not instantaneous, and may even develop some time after the end of the GAT-P:

I think probably the biggest thing it's done is help me see what happened to me, as an adult... It's made me see things. Probably, I've been so confused and mixed up that it's kind of made things clearer. And I value myself more as a person, and I feel I'm worth something, which to be honest I didn't before... The two months or so since the group has finished, I didn't see it at the time but it's proved to me that I was getting some strength from the sessions.

For one woman, the new way of seeing meant that for the first time she was able to separate out the abuser and his wife in her mind. She had previously blamed the wife for the abuse because of sexual difficulties in the couple's relationship. She was able to trace her shift in perspective to one particular activity in the sessions (see pp.161–163):

It was doing that 'trial', I think they separated. It was like say before, you've got them all sort of stuck together. I thought the glue came undone, they were apart. I've always said any time in the last few years when I've talked about them, that it was [his wife's] fault, that if she'd been normal – there was never any sex apparently in their marriage – and if she'd been the sort of woman who would have thought that was wrong – she didn't, she thought it was good, thought how good he was – that he wouldn't have been like that. I mean, now I can accept that this is not so. I think both of these two people have got problems with this, and that's attracted them to each other. It's not one caused the other, they were like that anyway.

This awareness of separateness may also enable some women to realise that not all men are evil:

I'm still very wary of men but that isn't altogether a bad thing anyway, I don't think. I do try not to tar everyone with the same brush, which I did at one stage.

One research participant spoke of her shifted position regarding the abuser (a father-figure). This shift appears to have included some distance, which facilitated clearer vision:

I was going through a stage then when I wanted my dad back. I mean, I sit still and cry about it. You know, I wanted him to be like he was when I was very young. I don't feel I need that now. You know, I think I can stand back and look at him for the person he was, good or bad. It doesn't get me either as upset, or as desolate, or as angry... Sometimes I've thought, was it me, but there's no strength to that thought now, it is diminishing. And I don't feel that I was responsible for that.

For one woman, the change in perspective seems to have been associated with a reduction in her symptoms, namely 'flashbacks', during which survivors of trauma re-experience events as if they were happening in the present:

> I used to get a lot of flashbacks and voices, and things like that...coming back and saying that it was my fault. I'm in control from him now, I can control him if he comes back. I can turn around and say: 'Get lost! Not part of me any more. Can't hurt me any more.'

Another woman clearly describes the link between being witnessed and gaining a new perspective:

> I think on reflection it's made me realise I can trust people more and that people are not going to reject me as much as I thought they were going to... I'm beginning to see that life is more of a two-way thing instead of a one-way. It's give and take, really.

At times, the new perspective includes an acceptance that

> what happened, happened. No one can take that away... I'll never forget what's happened, but I think I'll learn to live with it.

The speaker seems, in accepting this fact, to be contemplating the final task of the recovery process, laying to rest the abuse, or achieving some kind of inner resolution. She knew that she had not arrived yet at that point, but had hope that she would eventually do so.

For some women, this self-acceptance means the end of a search for memories that may still remain unavailable:

> I'm glad I've blocked it out, and I hope the memory never comes back, because I think it's better not to have that memory.

This is a subtly different position from that of burial. The woman concerned had by now completed the GAT-P, had retrieved some important memories, dealt with them and decided quite consciously on her new position. This was not a position of denial, but of acceptance. It therefore links with the final task of laying to rest the abuse.

The ability to gain a new perspective, to understand, to achieve change on the cognitive level is probably more important in the long run than catharsis, as one woman reflected: 'I think it's more to do with the understanding of it than sort of getting it out.'

Occasionally, there is a realisation that not all of the survivor's childhood was bad: there may have been pockets during which she felt quite happy, as some of the research participants discovered to their delight. Sadly, this is not the case for all women who were abused as children.

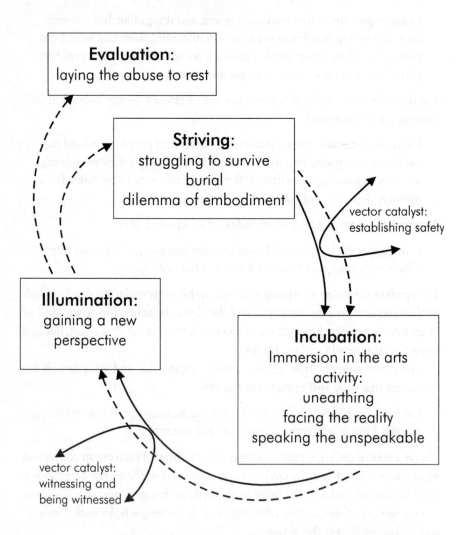

Figure 3.1 – A creative model of recovery from the trauma of child sexual abuse

The cognitive changes identified by several research participants appeared to occur often as a flash of inspiration, although many also developed slowly over time. The difference between these two kinds of experiences may represent two different forms of learning. The notion of flashes of inspiration fits most easily with the creative process discussed in Chapter 2 and represented diagrammatically in relation to the recovery process in Figure 3.1. The second form of cognitive change appears to be the result of an apparently slower, equally important, though less seductive process, which may be perceived only with hindsight. It could be argued that cognitive change is a goal of all therapy. In most cases, this appeared to precede important behavioural change for the women I spoke with. In other therapeutic approaches, for example assertiveness training, behavioural change may be achieved before cognitive change, and is used to reinforce new self-concepts.

Evaluation: laying the abuse to rest and gaining temporal and spatial distance

While it could be argued that recovery from trauma is a growthful process, which ends only with death (if then), there does appear to be a stage which I have labelled, using words contributed by research participants, laying to rest. This stage is interesting because it seems to mirror, in a much more healthy way, the burial experienced at the start of the journey. Burial quite often implies a burial in the body, resulting in somatisation, substance misuse, self-injury and numbing of sensations and affects. Laying to rest, on the other hand, implies a distance from the body, so that the physical self can be reclaimed and dis-identified from the experience of abuse. Moreover, there is a temporal distance as the abuse becomes a memory in the true sense (as in the adult state), which can be accessed at will but is not intrusive and ever-present (as it would be in the child state).

For one woman, the metaphor of laying to rest had a very specific meaning. She had lost her baby in upsetting circumstances, and mourning the child through a symbolic ceremony in the group was the most important thing she achieved in the programme:

> the one thing I did do was to put [my baby] to rest and I have done that and I feel a lot happier for it. I feel that was the one thing that I wanted to do, and I did it... Before the group...practically all the time I used to think of [my baby] a hell of a lot. But [she] is resting now and I go and see,

and I go and put flowers on... I just think: My little girl is gone, and it wasn't my fault.

Several of the research participants referred to this particular woman's piece of work in the group. Although none of the women made conscious connections to the possibility that they might also be grieving for their own inner abused 'child self', this possibility was explored during clinical supervision by the therapists. One woman had this to say:

It's having a child and knowing, well thinking you know how [the other woman in the group] must have felt. And feeling the injustice of it all, and hoping that in the end she would be able to put it behind her and lay her to rest properly. The whole idea was to help [her], but it really affected me because of having a child myself and just the whole thing.

One of the things that another woman from a different group managed to achieve during the programme was to grieve and let go of a dead loved one, who in some ways was linked with her abuse but whom she had loved dearly. She was not able to say whether anything specific happened in the sessions to precipitate this. The actual process occurred at home:

I was having a really bad do at home, and I could actually see him in his coffin, in the lounge, and I lay next to his coffin. And I spoke to him and stroked him, and told him that I was letting go and everything. I really cried and really grieved for days and days, and I've felt better since then.

This is not dissimilar to the process described by another woman, concerning the memory of her father trying to harm her as a little girl, which she recalled during a group session when she chose something from a box of objects (see Chapter 6) provided by the therapists:

at the time, it really did affect me for about a week. And I was really crying and crying, and sobbing and sobbing. And I kept having nightmares about it and it kept going through my mind. But then after that, a couple of weeks afterwards, I felt as though I'd worked it through, really.

Several women referred to an emerging sense of self. One group named themselves 'the chrysalis group', which seems metaphorically and archetypally to reflect this process:

positive in the developing sense, was the idea of the butterfly, and the chrysalis.

Another woman described the emerging self using a different metaphor:

> I was more in touch with that me that was now getting more chance to grow. It was as if the little seed of my life which was me and had been kept down by all this stuff on top of it, was beginning to break through all this stuff. And I really grew a lot in two or three weeks, I felt.

This statement is reminiscent of one woman's suggestion that the good is buried along with the bad. She felt that it is only with the unearthing that the good can begin to grow. Like the chrysalis image, her metaphor implies something new and beautiful emerging, after being hidden. Interestingly, this emergence does not mean a denial or abandonment of the old self, but an integration and transformation:

> it's like being tuned to how I used to be, but moving on with that broader horizon, if you like.

A broader horizon implies a greater sense of space and a clearer view, which can be achieved only by viewing at a distance, and higher up.

One woman said that during the GAT-P sessions she at first had still felt like the child who was abused, but that gradually the 'adult self' took over. For a second woman, the fact that she is a mother herself enabled her to begin during therapy to see things from a mother's perspective, and to grieve for the abused child. A third woman revealed, at the research meeting during which I presented my tentative findings, that she had previously felt as if she had several selves, each with her own personality and way of moving. She was now beginning to discover an integrated self, and emphasised that she had not killed any of these selves off; they had begun to become one self.

When one woman, during her clinical review/research interview, examined some of the images she had created, she was struck by how some of them seemed

> quite far away, actually. It's been and gone and done. But there's some of it that isn't, it's still sort of everyday.

Paradoxically, there seems to be a need for some level of self-acceptance concerning the pace of recovery before the survivor can begin to experience this distancing from her own experience:

> I thought I was going to be ill for about eight weeks. It took quite a long time, but I don't feel uncomfortable about that... If it's taken this time, it's taken this time, and that's all there is to it. They can't shoot me, can they?

This level of self-acceptance inevitably implies an acceptance that therapy is no 'quick fix'. For this woman, it included the awareness that: 'I can't really put it to rest. I'm not ready to put it to rest at the moment.' Another woman was aware that

> there's a lot of things that happened with [one abuser]. I've never really spoken about that with the group and there are certain aspects of that I need to lay to rest.

Also, regarding the other abuser, about whom she had disclosed in group sessions, the speaker wanted to find a position that would enable her not to be

> looking over my shoulder, or avoiding certain places at certain times, constantly looking round every time I'm in the street. Because I don't want to live like that.

One woman felt that once she had attended an assertiveness class following the GAT-P, she would be able to put the abuse behind her:

> I feel you've got to a stage where you've got to, you know, say right, I've got to let go and get on with my life. I think I've sort of covered everything that I needed to in the group.

There comes a time when there is a need to leave active therapy about the abuse behind:

> I feel you've…got to, you know, say right, I've got to let go and get on with my life.

Before this can occur, the survivor must inevitably accept both herself and the process. Central to the stage of laying the abuse to rest is the sense of a future. Since hopelessness about the future is one of the risk factors associated with parasuicidal behaviour (MacLeod, Williams and Linehan 1992), this development is a particularly important one:

> I know there is a future for me. God knows when it's gonna happen, but before I didn't have one, or I felt I didn't have one.

> I don't know exactly where I'm going, but I'm not as frightened of the thought of moving forward as I was.

For some survivors, the distance is tangibly represented by a new determination not to see the abuser, with whom she may previously have been in contact. For example, two of the research participants drastically reduced contact with the abuser (a father-figure), despite expectations within the families that each would continue to behave as a dutiful daughter.

While the concept of laying to rest may be a useful one in contemplating an end to the recovery process, it is possible in fact that there is no end as such, as one woman implied: 'It's just a journey, isn't it? We've done a bit, and I'm continuing.'

On the face of it, this knowledge of an ongoing journey may seem rather depressing, unless one takes a similar view of life itself. To the extent that everyone (usually) grows as a human being throughout the individual's lifetime, the concept of an endless journey seems both accurate and welcome. But it raises the question: when does the survivor know that she no longer needs therapy? The answer to this may lie in the extent to which her mental health symptoms disrupt her life. For one woman, who had been having flashbacks prior to the GAT-P, the sense of distance she experienced was observable. Her memories, like the memories of other people who suffer intrusive imagery associated with post-traumatic states (Hossack and Bentall 1996), were like a videotape replay. The 'videotape' could be triggered by television programmes, discussion in the group sessions, and so on:

> The nightmares and the recurrence of it are almost like a video that you put on replay, so that it keeps going through and through and through, to the point where you almost get fed up of it going through.

However, some of this research participant's worst memories were not like a 'video replay' that she was watching. Rather, it was as if she was in the scene, which was happening to her at that moment. She described this to me when I met with her to give her a copy of her interview transcript. She said that when the CATs technique worked well, she went back to being in the situation, effectively reliving it. The difference between this experience and that of the awful memories which occurred when she was alone (and that of the abuse itself) was that during group sessions she was aware of someone being there with her, that is witnessing. This enabled her to sob, which she could also do when watching the 'video' memories, but not when reliving them alone as a participant. The reason for the suppression of her tears was that her father had abused her more violently when, as a child, she had cried. After going through the tears and the pain approximately thirty times, she said, the event became a mere memory. She threw further light on this process at a research group meeting: the creative arts allowed her to express and channel her feelings. They provided a way of speaking which was cathartic. But it was the witnessing of this, the acceptance of it by others that allowed her to change her perceptions. Without the witnessing, she would still have gone home in a better state, having released feelings and expressed something that needed expressing, but for the cognitive and behavioural change to occur the experience of being witnessed was essential. This, she explained, was because she had never had the experience of being witnessed (benevolently) by a parent when young. For her, both the arts and the witnessing were essential components in her recovery.

This particular research participant attributed many of the problems she had experienced to the fact that the abuser had threatened awful things if she ever told, and so the reality of the abuse had been

> stored inside us like a time bomb inside. And it's really how you get from that time bomb inside, how you get it out without hurting yourself, without killing yourself through getting it out. But it's the getting it out – and once you get a bit of it out and you work it through over and over again, the pain goes less and less from it. 'Til at the end you think, no I don't want to talk that through again… It's in the past, it happened in the past. And it goes back into its space in the past. And it happened in the past, and it's there and it'll always be there. But it goes from present to past. And that's what that's gone now, into the past.

Here, she seems to be making a reference to burial followed by unearthing, a process which is seen as potentially dangerous and must be made safe. The survivor is then able to speak about what happened so that, after going through the process many times, the abuse is laid to rest. This description of the process bears some relationship to Hossack and Bentall's (1996) cognitive method for dealing with intrusive imagery. She was clear that what made her symptoms (nightmares and flashbacks) worse for a while, was the fact that she was confronting or facing what had happened to her as a child. This was made possible by the safety of being in a group situation with other people who were also confronting issues (the group witness), but also crucially the safety she experienced in her relationship with her key worker.

It is possible to view the recovery process not only as a creative process, but also within a developmental framework. There are some analogies to the process described by Mahler (1979), as the infant progresses from a merged state with the attachment object (in this case a negative attachment), towards separation – individuation. This analysis might also provide some explanation for the report by more than one research participant that recovery meant the discovery of an adult self, which could now have a future.

Summary

I have outlined in this chapter my model for recovery from CSA. I described the model in detail as a narrative, using the words of the women who participated in my doctoral research to illustrate key concepts. I have also shown the model diagrammatically, in a simplified form (Figure 3.1). The model is viewed as a fluid, convenient fiction rather than solid fact, and invites further investigation. The process has been conceptualised as a creative spirallic journey, although this is acknowledged as a simplification of a very complex process. The general trend appears to be a developmental one, which could be said to mirror ontological development in that the self becomes more integrated, essentially adult with access to the 'inner child'. The memories of abuse similarly recede into the past and are no longer buried within the body.

Pertinent to the second part of this book is the information gleaned about the potential usefulness of the CATs in treatment planning for survivors of CSA. The specific usefulness appears to lie in

- their ability to unearth unconscious material

- their containing and distancing properties, when planned and used with this in mind

- the potential for generating an image, which can be faced, witnessed and appraised

- the sense that the creation 'speaks for' the survivor, either without the need for the more familiar use of language as discourse, or facilitating this.

I remain cautious in appraising the worth of any therapeutic system. There is evidence in my research that the CATs are very powerful tools that may assist the survivor in recovery. However, like many other treatment approaches, if used without the necessary sense of safety, they may lead to deterioration. Moreover, not everyone finds it easy to use creative modalities.

The role of the group as witness has been highlighted, which lends support to the suggestion that group therapy at some stage is useful for survivors of CSA. The need for strong support via a key worker has also been emphasised. The risk of eliciting false memories was discussed in Chapter 2, although it has been acknowledged that this is unlikely in the hands of a trained and adequately supervised creative arts therapist. All of these issues should be borne in mind when reading the second part of this book.

Note

1   I am grateful to my brother-in-law, Mel Hales, for helping me to consider this in terms of chemical reactions, and to my son, Joseph Meekums, for coming up with the term 'vector catalyst' once I explained my ideas to him.

PART TWO

The Practice

Introduction to Part Two

I have written this book with the mental health context in mind. This is because much of my experience of working with adult survivors of abuse has been gained in adult mental health within the British NHS. You are invited to adapt the material to your own context. This should not be a difficult task, as I have written cautiously, with the most fragile client in mind and it is easier to adapt from more to less fragile clients than vice versa.

Group therapy appears to provide one crucial element in recovery from CSA trauma, namely what Yalom (1975) calls 'universality', the sense that one is not alone. This cannot so easily be provided through individual therapy. Other experiences can assist the development of universality, for example structured bibliotherapy and careful exposure to certain television programmes (provided that neither of these will be retraumatising for the client). Group therapy provides an opportunity to explore differences and similarities in the experience of each individual group member, within a structured, contained environment. Despite this, there is a risk that betrayal issues will emerge in the group dynamics. When betrayal does arise, it must be handled carefully by sensitive, experienced therapists. For this reason, self-help groups are not indicated for survivors of CSA in mental health settings, although they may be useful for those survivors whose level of symptomatology does not warrant referral to a mental health service.

The sense of identity between group members appears to strengthen the role of 'witness'. While therapists can provide this function in individual therapy, the role of the group is subtly different. In the group setting, the role of witness seems to be to do with a reframing of personal identity from lone victim-child to collective powerful-adult. Many of the women who moved on from the group arts therapies programme in my study internalised an image of the group, which strengthened and supported them. Had the group not been time-limited, this might have operated less well, potentially fostering a continued identity with the abuse rather than supporting the process of moving on. I am making the assumption in the second part of this book that you are intending to run a time-limited group, of about twenty sessions. If you wish to vary from this format, you will need to adapt the advice given to your own needs.

CHAPTER 4

Setting Up the Group

Introduction

It is important to plan carefully before advertising the group to potential referrers. You will need to consider such factors as location, time, day, length of session, number of sessions, number of participants, referral criteria, number and gender of therapists, techniques to be offered, equipment needed, goals of the group, and so on.

For many of these questions, there are no right or wrong answers. The eventual solution will be a best fit between what is desirable and the resources available.

Clinical supervision

Supervision often is the last thing which co-workers plan when setting up a new therapy group. However, it is one of the most important considerations. You need to choose a supervisor with whom you both feel comfortable, who knows about groups and about CSA if possible, and who can be supportively challenging, in particular in helping you to confront possible splitting in the group and between yourselves. I suggest meeting with your supervisor at least once during the planning stage, then at regular intervals (monthly is usually adequate) during the programme, and once after the group has ended.

Location of group meetings

Ideally, a room should be sought for group meetings which can be structured for maximum therapeutic effect and which is located in an accessible area for public transport. You may need toilets near to the room, which can be accessed by wheelchair users. You will also need to consider privacy. Can voices be heard outside the room? Are the windows overlooked? Privacy is very important in any kind of therapy, but this is even more the case when the topic is a sensitive one, and when the experiences of the participants have previously been marked by serious invasions of privacy, as in the case of CSA.

Deciding a time and day

The time and day of the session will be determined to some extent by worker and room availability, but the group will not recruit if you do not also make some allowances for the commitments of your participants. For example, many groups run best between the hours of 10 a.m. and 2 p.m. This allows for parents of young schoolchildren to attend. It is often best to schedule the sessions within term time, for similar reasons. If, on the other hand, most potential participants are at work, you may wish to consider an evening group. The length of each session may depend on the modalities you emphasise. For example, art materials require a little more organisation within the session than drama and movement. Many participants will feel that, no matter how long the session, they wish it was longer. Others will feel that they wish it was shorter. I have found that one and a half to two hours, depending on the size of the group, is about right.

Number of sessions

A programme of twenty sessions with a closed group satisfies the current trend towards short-term, focused interventions, while enabling some in-depth work. However, in order to provide this, it is essential that the women have all had prior disclosure work in individual therapy with a key worker (usually social worker or psychiatric nurse if in a mental health setting) in whom trust has been established. Ideally, the same key worker should remain involved during the groupwork programme, and liase with the group therapists. This can be a tall order, as not all key workers have the necessary therapeutic skills. Those who do have therapy skills might not be able to make good use of them due to service priorities for case management and throughput.

An alternative is, as den Herder and Redner (1991) have found to be effective, a rolling programme of closed groups. These can admit new members at the start of each programme as others leave, yet enable each woman to stay as long as she wishes up to a maximum of sixty sessions. The rolling closed group programme allows for the sense of safety and shared purpose that can be generated through a closed group, while allowing for some flexibility. The other advantage of the rolling programme is that the group therapists can evaluate each programme before commencing the next, thus continually improving service quality. The big disadvantage is that some purchasers would question the provision of sixty sessions of group therapy on financial grounds. More outcome studies are needed to demonstrate the effectiveness and 'best value' or otherwise of the different options.

Number of group members

The number of participants is probably best set at around six to eight. Any larger than this, and the women could feel too overwhelmed by the number in the room. This could inhibit group discussion and lead to a high drop-out rate. Fewer than five, and the group is in danger of folding if more than one person drops out. A small group may also suffer from insufficient contributions by group members acting as witnesses and informants for each other.

Publicising the group and getting referrals

You will need at least twice as many referrals than the number of group members envisaged, and possibly up to four or five times as many. Your referral information is crucial in keeping this gap as small as possible. You could consider offering a consultancy service to people who are thinking of making referrals. Referrers would usually rather discuss their clients before completing complicated forms that might lead to nothing (from their point of view). Sometimes whole teams will allow you to visit and talk to them, so that they can ask general questions. You will need to be confident before suggesting this!

One of the problems you may encounter is that individual key workers/ therapists are only human. They may be reticent about referring clients to group therapy, preferring to contain all therapeutic change within the individual therapy relationship. However, in reality no one exists without multiple influences on their life. Other therapists/key workers may be wary of either the modality (arts therapies) or of group therapy *per se*. Such wariness may be due either to a lack of personal experience, or to adverse experiences as either client or therapist.

Equally legitimate is the concern that the group therapists may work in ways that conflict with the goals of the individual therapist or key worker. It is therefore important to reassure any referrer that the group therapists wish to work together with the team, in the interests of the client. Multi-disciplinary reviews can be built into this framework.

One of the important 'selling' points about group therapy is that it enables survivors to feel less isolated. The enormous benefit in meeting other survivors, and realising that one is neither alone nor mad, cannot be precisely replicated in any other way, so far as I know.

One of the mistakes often made by group therapists is to take 'all comers', in order to get enough people for a group. This, in my experience, leads to a high drop-out rate. As I got better at referral and assessment, my drop-out rate fell from about 50 per cent to about 15 per cent. You need to decide both inclusion and exclusion criteria (see the assessment section, pp.126–135).

I find that the goals of the group are best expressed in any referral publicity in terms that mean something to psychiatrists and key workers. It is important to consider the problems faced by workers who have case management or medical responsibilities. In the mental health services, many CSA survivors present with co-morbidity, with or without a diagnosis of a personality disorder. Referral information will need to reflect the particular concerns of the referrer whatever the setting, including self-referral in community settings. The aims of the group can and should then be reviewed and refined to be relevant to the group participants, both at assessment as discussed below and at the first group meeting as explained in Chapter 5. These refined goals can be used to evaluate progress, and thus to evaluate the usefulness of the intervention, provided that they are stated in operational terms that are easily identified and measured.

An example of a referral information sheet is given in Figure 4.1

Co-work

Wherever possible, two group therapists should work together throughout the planning, assessment, therapy and evaluation stages. I see no reason why some sessions should not be run by just one of the two therapists, provided that notice is given where possible to the group members, and that this constitutes no more than one-fifth, say, of the sessions in total. The co-therapy relationship allows for group members to project different roles onto each of the therapists, which can be tested out and worked with. It also provides support for the therapists in facing group dynamics. The experience of abuse can be replayed in the group dynamics; group therapists need to be aware of this possibility. When disclosures are made within the group, the co-work relationship can provide additional support to clinical supervision, in

Figure 4.1 – Referral information sheet

New Therapy Group for Female Survivors of Child Sexual Abuse

Location

The group will be held in the newly refurbished creative therapies studio.

Times and day

We are hoping to schedule the group in order to fit in with the commitments of people who are assessed as needing this group.

Format of the group

We will offer a time-limited format, 20 sessions, with a closed group of up to 8 women.

Group therapists

The group will be run by Bonnie Meekums, Head Dance Movement Therapist, and Someone Smith, a Community Psychiatric Nurse with some training in art therapy.

Referral criteria

This group is open to women who are already clients of the mental health service, have disclosed a history of child sexual abuse, and have spent at least six months in disclosure work with a therapeutically-orientated mental health worker. In addition, the key worker will need to contract to maintain regular weekly or fortnightly contact throughout the groupwork programme and for a minimum of three months afterwards, in order to assist the client in processing and integrating change.

Aims and methods

We will be making use of the approach researched by Bonnie Meekums and reported in her book *Creative Group Therapy for Women Survivors of Child Sexual Abuse*. Our main aim is to enable the women to disclose the 'relevant account' of their abuse, in a supportive group atmosphere, and to begin to attribute different meanings to this so that they can move on.

Liaison

We intend to keep regular contact with the key worker and psychiatrist, reporting any perceived changes in mental state at the earliest opportunity. We will also send you copies of our assessment and discharge report for the client referred. If we have any concerns about the safety of the client or any other individual connected with them, e.g. a child, we will also report this to you as a matter of urgency. The client will be made aware of these limits to confidentiality. We would welcome receipt of a copy of your care plan, and will discuss any concerns you may have about how the therapy fits into this. We are also available to attend multidisciplinary reviews.

Where to send referrals

Please make all referrals using the enclosed referral form and send these to: Bonnie Meekums, PhD, SRDMT, Any Hospital, Any Street, Any Town. Alternatively, you may telephone Bonnie before completing the form on: 0200 0000000.

enabling therapists to process their own responses. I confess that I have not co-worked with a man on any of the CSA groups that I have run, although I know male therapists who have done this work with extreme sensitivity and I have had some clinical supervision from a man. The gender balance may, in the end, be determined by availability but there are obvious advantages and disadvantages to each scenario of same-gender and mixed-gender therapists. The one combination I would not recommend is two men when facilitating a women survivors' group. While this book deals directly with group therapy for women survivors, there is also the potential for mixed groups for some clients in certain settings, and mixed-gender therapists may well work best for these. Most of my clients would say that they could not contemplate having a male therapist or working in a mixed group, at least early in their recovery. Some might find a mixed-gender environment useful at a later stage in their therapy, in order to re-evaluate their responses to men.

It is important for co-workers to spend time preparing together, not just to discuss techniques and approaches, but also to think honestly about the strengths and resources each brings to the work, including the potential conflicts which might arise. Experienced co-workers will know their weaknesses, whether that is for example to rush in too early with reflections during the session, thus blocking one's co-worker, or to tend to leave leadership to the other therapist, both in and out of the session. It is important to decide who is responsible for what. Even the question of whose turn it is to photocopy more recording sheets or to wash up the coffee cups can be sources of conflict. It is important to discuss what each of you wants from the other, what each feels able to contribute, and what strengths and weaknesses each of you brings. It is useful to give permission to each other to point out failings when they arise, or to air responses to each other's behaviour. After all, you will hope that the group members are honest with each other! Once all of this is aired, and a few shortcomings made visible within an atmosphere of human acceptance, it may also be important for each of you to discuss how this work affects you. Such discussions might include sharing sexual histories. Let there be no mistake about it, it is not possible to do this work unless you are prepared to self-reflect, and have worked through your own issues around power and sexuality to some degree. A good supervisor will pick up on this anyway, if it becomes an issue in relation to the group, and it is far better for you if you have done some talking between yourselves first. Related issues like food, substance use and relationships may also need tackling. Having said all of this, you do not need to spend long on this. One way I have done this in the past quite successfully with co-workers is to list the themes and issues brought by group participants on paper. I use boxes to represent each of the group members and the two co-workers, then draw lines that connect these issues to each of the co-workers. This requires minimal self-disclosure, while flagging up the issues, and can provide a framework for further discussion if required. The exercise is best done following assessment, as the themes brought by each woman will be more obvious at that stage than earlier. I present a hypothetical version of this in Figure 4.2.

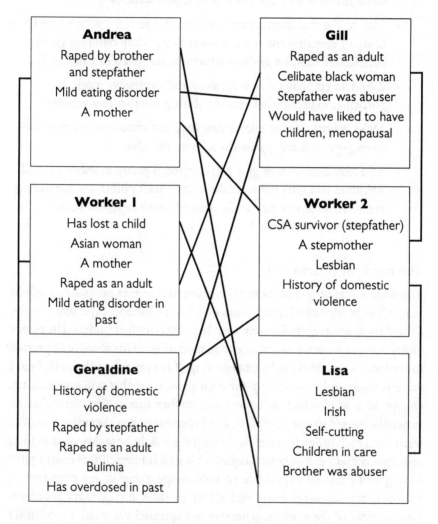

Andrea

Raped by brother and stepfather

Mild eating disorder

A mother

Gill

Raped as an adult

Celibate black woman

Stepfather was abuser

Would have liked to have children, menopausal

Worker 1

Has lost a child

Asian woman

A mother

Raped as an adult

Mild eating disorder in past

Worker 2

CSA survivor (stepfather)

A stepmother

Lesbian

History of domestic violence

Geraldine

History of domestic violence

Raped by stepfather

Raped as an adult

Bulimia

Has overdosed in past

Lisa

Lesbian

Irish

Self-cutting

Children in care

Brother was abuser

Figure 4.2 – Co-work preparation

Safety issues

It is important to consider carefully the clients' sense of safety. This appears to be best achieved by paying attention to the following guidelines:

- Group members who have complex mental health symptoms (including co-morbidity with or without the diagnosis of a personality disorder) should have had previous individual therapy, and should maintain ongoing contact with a key worker.

- The therapy room must afford confidentiality and is improved by some division into discussion and action sections.

- Plan to use therapeutic structures in early sessions which provide a sense of containment and empowerment, while building group cohesion. Examples of these structures are given in Chapter 5.

- Avoid an emphasis on exploratory and expressive work, in particular expressive movement, during the first few sessions.

- Make it very clear to clients that they can choose whether or not to engage with any particular activity on offer.

- You may also wish to give each potential group member a list of helplines and telephone numbers or contact points, for use during crisis. This list will be locally defined; some suggestions are provided in Appendix 3.

The need for eclecticism

The wide range of responses to therapeutic techniques necessitates eclecticism. Choice is crucial for survivors of CSA, childhood experience having denied them any real choice over what happened to their bodies. The opportunity to try out a range of activities and modalities in the absence of pressure to conform is thus likely to be empowering. If the range is sufficiently broad, there is likely to be something for each participant that will enable her to engage at a level which is appropriate to her needs. Arts therapists are generally trained in one discipline, but experienced arts therapists can often learn from each other, in order to develop their skills base. My own guiding principle is that I use only techniques with which I myself feel comfortable, having had personal experience of their usage either in my own therapy and/or in training workshops. Verbal therapy skills are necessary in order to process some of the material generated or expressed via creative modalities; verbalisation appears to aid the re-evaluation and integration of experience.

Therapist style

It is crucial that therapists are competent (Mitchell *et al*. 1977). General therapeutic skills should be second-nature. These include non-possessive warmth, empathy and genuineness (Rogers 1957) to enhance the therapeutic relationship. In addition, it is important to address through one's actions, the survivor's tendency to expect to be judged and abused. This means showing that one is not shocked by what is being disclosed; making it clear that the survivor is not to blame for the abuse; and assuring the survivor that she is in charge, within agreed boundaries.

Boundaries

Therapeutic boundaries are important with any client group. It is sometimes helpful to remind ourselves of how and why we keep boundaries. I offer my thoughts on this.

What are therapeutic boundaries?

Examples of therapeutic boundaries include:

- a set number of sessions
- starting and finishing on time
- keeping confidentiality
- avoidance of talking about one's own personal life, except when this is in the service of the therapy
- not offering therapy to a friend or family member
- not developing a friendship with a client
- not engaging in sexual activity with a client
- making the space safe, i.e. not intruded upon by others during the session
- not leaving confidential material lying around
- not having photographs of your own children on the desk
- not giving clients your home telephone number
- having an ex-directory telephone number.

Why do we make boundaries in therapy?

It is possible that not all of the above list would be used by all therapists. For example, whether or not to register one's telephone number as ex-directory is a matter of personal choice. However, at the other end of the scale it would be a disciplinary offence to have a sexual relationship with a client.

Boundaries provide a container for the therapy. They can create a sense of safety when addressing potentially overwhelming material. If a client knows that the therapist will not answer questions about her own family circumstances, this may feel extremely irritating and unfair at first, but eventually may make sense. For the therapist to engage in extensive self-disclosure would alter the balance and would therefore mean that roles became confused. It might reinforce the tendency of some survivors to become caretakers and thus avoid confronting their own needs for caretaking. Therapists must never use the therapeutic relationship in order to get their own needs met. I must emphasise that I do not believe in total avoidance of self-disclosure. The guiding question must always be: how will it help or hinder the therapy if I give my client this information about myself? I had one client who, after a few years of individual therapy with me, blurted out that I did not know what it was like to be the client. I casually informed her that all therapists have to go through their own therapy, an intervention which while fairly small for me, had huge significance for her. Instantly I became more human to her, and therefore more trustworthy, and she was able to begin a new phase of disclosure work. Some therapists would argue that my intervention would have been even more effective if I had first explored what it might mean to her if I did or did not know first hand what it feels like to be the client. The potential therapeutic advantages of such questioning must be weighed up against the real possibility that it could be viewed negatively by the client, thus damaging the therapeutic alliance.

The issue of time-keeping is less straightforward. Some therapists (and clients) argue that it is difficult to put a time limit on disclosure work. My own experience is, that if the survivor knows that she only has to face this material for a set time each week, she can cope more easily than if disclosure is a seemingly never-ending event (the same argument applies to time-limited programmes). One of the main tasks for some survivors is to learn to speak out; some women will avoid disclosing until the last minute in a session, to avoid having to say too much, and that is their right. The therapist should always be vigilant to this possibility when she is feeling guilty about calling time!

The main reason why boundaries are so important in working with survivors of CSA, is that the child who was abused was subjected to an invasion of her body boundaries, which threatened her very sense of self. At the same time, she may have had to conform to rigid boundaries and rules of a punitive nature. The restructuring of benevolent boundaries, while it may at first remind the survivor of the punitive boundaries she encountered as a child, will eventually allow for a reworking of this early experience.

Equipment

Figure 4.3 gives some suggestions for equipment that may be useful in group sessions.

Figure 4.3 – Equipment list

Large soft balls, e.g. foam footballs (can be bought in good toy shops)

Large stretch lycra cloth

Large pieces of very wide elastic, knotted (one white and one black to maximise symbolic possibilities)

Large pieces of coloured sugar paper

A variety of art media, including oil pastels, felt-tips, paints

Palettes, brushes, water containers, newspaper to protect the floor, cloth and bucket to mop it

Sound system with both CD and tape options

Assortment of recorded music

Soft toys

Boxes of small objects for projective work, including different containers; other symbolic objects (key, candle, snake, chain, plastic toy weapons, plastic toy sword for 'superhero' symbolism, sticking plaster, baby's feeding bottle, miniature loaf, masks – be inventive); toy furniture; toy transport including ambulance, police car, helicopter

Percussion instruments

Flip-chart paper and pens

Session structure

Figure 4.4 provides a sample session structure.

Figure 4.4 – Session structure

10 a.m. – Clients arrive and assemble on circle of chairs in carpeted area of room. 'Check-in', during which group members talk about their feelings concerning the previous session, and about anything which has arisen during the intervening week. Some clients may bring pieces of writing to share with the rest of the group.

10.20 a.m. – 'Warm-up', designed to act as preparation for the creative work of the session. May include, therefore, a physical warm-up of bodies, or the act of choosing art materials, arranging or choosing props, etc.

10.30 a.m. – Creative work. Usually takes place in the non-carpeted area.

11.00 a.m. – Group discussion, during which group members verbally process and share their feelings and reflections following the creative work. Takes place, usually on chairs, in the carpeted area.

11.50 a.m. – Closing, e.g. a circle dance or verbal activity such as choosing one thing to take symbolically from the session and one thing to leave behind.

12 p.m. – Clients leave.

Assessment

Introduction to assessment

Assessment is an important tool in the targeting of services so that the best outcomes are achieved. This goal is important not simply in order to save money for organisations, but to save distress for clients. Better assessment means that the therapy has a better chance of working.

Assessment for CSA group therapy is touched on only briefly in the existing literature, the most comprehensive attempts at defining assessment criteria being found in Sanderson (1990). Sanderson lists the following factors as important in the assessment process:

- the client's goals and expectations
- the ability to talk about the abuse and express affect
- the amount of previous therapy
- current health
- self-destructive behaviours
- motivation.

Sanderson (1990) lists the following factors as indicating a negative prognosis:

- volatile, aggressive, manic or disruptive behaviour
- the client being overly vulnerable or fragile
- drug and alcohol dependence
- active self-mutilation or suicidal behaviour
- psychosis, disorientation or heavy medication.

Sanderson's guidelines appear to have been derived from her own clinical experience and from similar literature, but they do not appear to have been the subject of systematic research.

The questions I use in assessment have been generated from my research study, my own clinical experience and Sanderson's (1990) suggestions. I am also greatly indebted to my colleague, Sue Fletcher (art therapist), for some of the material presented here. In particular, she contributed the guided imagery on landscape, and collaborated with me on drafting the assessment tools.

Screening

A screening form can be sent to referrers on receipt of a referral. Group therapists need to design their own form, in response to the needs of the setting. However, it is helpful if this can elicit the following information with respect to each client:

- the type and extent of previous help offered by statutory and other services
- the woman's previous experience of therapy groups
- reasons why group therapy is being sought at this time
- the woman's current state of health, both mental and physical

- any problems with written English, which might hinder the woman's use of creative writing techniques or demand a different approach from the therapists
- the relationship of the survivor to the abuser, nature of the abuse and apparent mental health outcomes
- the level of disclosure so far
- issues still to be addressed in therapy
- the level of both personal and professional support available to the woman
- some indication of motivation, and the help which might be needed with this
- problems such as child care or regular hospitalisations which might need to be addressed in order to maximise attendance
- the risks of treatment, including the level of decompensation experienced following important disclosures, risk of deliberate self-harm and risk of harm to others
- levels of dissociation, in particular whether the woman can maintain contact with external reality to the extent that she can hear and respond to the therapist's voice at all times
- special considerations, including ethnicity, sensory impairment, mobility issues
- any other information which the referrer feels is important.

On receipt of the screening form, an appointment for assessment can be offered provided that:

- there has been adequate previous disclosure work in individual therapy (a minimum of six months)
- levels of dissociation are not so high that the survivor would regress and be unable to maintain awareness of and response to the therapist's voice
- the level of risk is not such that there is a real possibility of suicide, harm to others or psychosis.

Assessment appointments

I suggest meeting with each woman on a minimum of two occasions for assessment purposes. The final meeting can be quite brief, and should be used to read out the assessment report so that the client gives informed consent to its use. The focus of assessment appointments should be:

- discussion of confidentiality issues
- clarification of information given on the screening form
- information dissemination concerning the group arts therapy programme
- exploration of the woman's feelings concerning the group context, confidentiality rules and use of creative media
- the suitability of the modalities being used, for example a guided imagery exercise to establish her ability to make use of visual imagery (see assessing the suitability of the modality, pp.131–133)
- establishment of realistic individualised aims for therapy
- existing ways of coping with distressing events, including any self-injurious behaviour
- completion of the self-assessment form (see p.132)
- the beginnings of the establishment of a therapeutic relationship.

CONFIDENTIALITY

Issues of confidentiality need to be carefully worked out; it helps if you have a prepared statement such as that in Figure 4.5, to give to clients at assessment.

RISK ASSESSMENT

A risk assessment should form part of any first contact with a client. This involves direct questioning about the individual's coping style, including hypothetical questions about how they might deal with either the emergence of distressing memories, or with hearing the disclosures of other group members. Such questioning can lead on to whether the person feels that she ever does anything to harm herself, intentionally or unintentionally. This could be about the kinds of relationships she has with others, how she uses food, substance use, and other actions including self-cutting. If there is evidence of self-harming, it is important to discover the following information: how recent the last incident was; how frequent they tend to be; under what circumstances they occur; and crucially what thoughts the person has or had at the time. For example, it is potentially more serious for a person to have taken just one extra paracetamol thinking this would kill her, than to have taken rather more than this in the hope simply to have a sleep from which she would wake. In other words, the intent to die (and planning of the means) is significant as an indicator that the person could eventually commit suicide. If risky behaviour tends to be associated with the emergence of distressing memories, disclosure-orientated therapy might be contra-indicated. Mitigating factors might include: more than six months since the last evidence of self-injury, or longer if this was a suicide attempt; evidence of new coping strategies; and experience of disclosure which did not result in self-harming or attempted suicide.

Figure 4.5 – Confidentiality statement

We respect your right to confidentiality. This means that we will only tell your key worker things that we feel it is important for her or him to know so that we can best help you. We will not gossip about you, nor will we talk to your family or friends except with your expressed wishes.

We will be having clinical supervision, which is not the same as supervision from a manager. The aim of clinical supervision is for us to provide the best possible service to you by discussing issues arising in the group with a trusted colleague, who also keeps confidentiality. This means that you can be assured that we reflect very carefully on the group in between sessions.

If we are concerned about you for any reason, we may need to contact someone in an emergency. We will try to do this with your consent where possible. If we become concerned that someone else is at risk, for example a child of whom you talk, we may need to contact someone outside of this service. Again, we will try to involve you in that decision but ultimately we have a legal responsibility to protect children and others, including yourself, when we can.

We do ask you to try not to talk about the other group members outside of the session. We understand that from time to time it may be necessary to do so with your therapist, but please do not identify other group members by name. We also ask group members not to discuss group issues with each other outside of the session. In this way, we can keep the whole group much safer.

We hope that you feel comfortable with all of this; please do air issues of concern with us. If you do not understand our reasons for anything stated here, do ask.

SELF-ASSESSMENT

The self-assessment form (Figure 4.6) is designed to elicit the client's cognitions and behaviours. Its use can be repeated at the end of therapy and again at follow-up appointments, offering a simple outcome measure. The version I present here has face validity, in that it is based on clinical experience of the issues which are pertinent to survivors. These are also supported by the literature reviewed in Chapter 1. I have found that, as the client self-assessment changes towards inclusion of the central column, other clinical indicators of recovery are also present. In other words, the proforma does seem to provide a rough measure of well-being. However, one word of caution in its use: no proforma should ever substitute for human interaction and discussion. While the test-retest methodology is considered to make good science, I have found that group participants are more able to reflect on their own experience following therapy than prior to it (Meekums 1990), meaning that the pre- and post-test design does not necessarily provide an entirely accurate picture of change. Having said that, I have found the tool to be useful in providing some visible evidence of change for the client.

If it is necessary to use a valid and reliable tool which has been thoroughly researched, Brière's Trauma Symptom Checklist (Brière and Runtz 1989) might be useful. The disadvantage of the better researched tools is that they tend to be longer and more stressful to use for the client. If the need is basically clinical rather than research or audit, I prefer to keep tools brief and user-friendly. The human dimension in assessment should never be over-looked.

ASSESSING THE SUITABILITY OF THE MODALITY

I have developed several ways to introduce the idea of dance movement therapy to people at assessment, without the need for the individual to feel too exposed. I explain each of these options to the client, asking her to choose just one as a 'taster'. The options include:

- throwing and catching a foam ball with the therapist (allowing for reflection on movement preferences and strengths)

- gentle stretches, led by the therapist (allowing for reflection on movement preferences and strengths)

- rubbing her own hands together, focusing on them, and allowing a positive association or memory to emerge. It is important to

Figure 4.6 – Self-assessment form

This is not a test and there are no 'right' or 'wrong' answers! It is a way for us and you to find out where you are in your recovery. Please circle the statement that most closely describes what you do with the feeling or behaviour listed in the left-hand column. For example, if you feel in control of your anger and able to express it at the right time and place, put a circle round 'in control'. If more than one column applies, please circle them both.

Feeling/behaviour			
Anger	take it out on myself in some way	able to express without losing control	take it out on others
Sadness	unable to cry or only cry alone	able to cry with someone I trust	out of control or very weepy
Enthusiasm	no enthusiasm	able to feel some enthusiasm	over the top or 'high'
Food	avoiding	eating well	over-eating
Memories of the abuse	buried	aware but not dominating my life	overwhelming or dominating life
Blame for the abuse	blame myself	blame the abuser	blame others
Sense of self-worth	I'm not an OK person	I'm an OK person	I'm a better person than others
Self-assertion	putting my needs last	putting my needs equal to others	putting my needs before others
Relationships	avoiding	balanced/co-operative	dependent
Hopes for the future	none	feel my hopes are realistic	feel my hopes are unrealistic

Please rate your own ability to self-assess: Poor • Fair • Good • Very Good

Please note any specific feeling/behaviour which you had difficulty in assessing:

....

....

Name ....   Date ....

Thank you for completing this form

emphasise that this is a positive memory, as the exercise provides a potentially powerful route to unconscious material

- manipulation of a small manikin doll into a position, then discussing the significance of this for the client

- brainstorming common phrases which make reference to bodies and body movement, for example 'put your back into it', then choosing one of these which has particular relevance to the individual (a development of this exercise being to demonstrate physically the movement metaphor).

The ability to engage with visual imagery can be assessed using the following guided visualisation (with acknowledgements to Sue Fletcher, art therapist):

I'd like to suggest you forget about what we've just been talking about for a while and just get a sense of the fact that you're here and sitting on that chair. I'm going to ask you to pay attention to pictures which form in your mind's eye. If you want to, close your eyes or fix your gaze on something, but I'd like you to just get a sense of how you feel now, the fact that you are sitting on a chair ... and imagine that inside your head there's a screen. To start with, just wipe the screen clean. You don't need to remember anything. Very gradually, I'd like you to watch that screen and watch an image, a landscape appear on it, the kind of landscape that you feel you're in now that feels right for how you are now. Have a look and see where you are in the landscape. Are you by yourself? What's the weather like? Can you smell anything, touch anything? And when you've got a real feel of that scene, fix it in your mind and bring it back with you to where you are now ... Can you tell us about your landscape?

I have less experience of assessing for dramatherapy, but I imagine that it would be possible to devise a similar exercise without asking the person to actually get up out of the chair and act. They might, for example, talk about what they watch on the television, which books they have read, stories they remember from childhood and so on. This could lead to a discussion of the roles in those settings, which ones feel familiar and which ones the client would like to be able to experience.

MAKING A DECISION

Following the two assessment appointments, the group therapists can complete an assessment checklist (Figure 4.7) and rate the woman's prognosis as either hopeful, less hopeful or hopeless. It is helpful to arrive at

Figure 4.7 – Assessment checklist

Name of client .... Date of assessment ....

Names of assessors ....

Positive factors (tick those present and add comments in brackets if relevant)
1. Has had at least six months' preparatory disclosure work
2. Ongoing therapeutic 1:1 support
3. Can maintain present reality
4. Internal locus of control
5. Able to set realistic goals
6. Able to see advantages to group setting
7. Can engage with (creative) media for work and see potential usefulness
8. Physical health good or problems unlikely to disrupt attendance/concentration severely
9. Adaptive coping strategies for stress

Negative factors (tick those present and add comments in brackets where relevant)
1. Psychotic, disorientated or heavily medicated
2. Referral or assessment data suggest that client may seek 1:1 attention to the exclusion of being able to identify as a member of the group
3. Referrer or group therapists assess the client as likely to be volatile, aggressive or manic in the group
4. Suicidal or engaged in self-harming behaviour which presents real risk to life
5. Drug or alcohol dependent, to the extent that this interrupts therapy appointments/ability to engage in therapy
6. Anorexic or bulimic (acute, or chronic but severe with no previous progress made)
7. Very withdrawn, i.e. unable to respond to questions
8. Major life transitions likely, e.g. birth, court proceedings, divorce, frequent house moves
9. Child care or other problems likely to interrupt attendance
10. Pattern of mental health crises requiring regular hospitalisation

Analysis (circle 1, 2 or 3)
1. **Hopeful prognosis**. Some permanent gain expected. All of the positives present, no negatives
2. **Less hopeful prognosis**. Gains may be smaller, transitory, or only maintained by further therapeutic intervention. Fewer positives and/or one or more negatives (but positives 1, 2 and 3 present and negatives 1, 2 and 3 absent)
3. **Hopeless prognosis**. No apparent gains expected. Absence of positive factors 1, 2 or 3 and/or presence of negative factors 1, 2 or 3.

NB: No place should be offered if prognosis is hopeless, as this may even have a counter-therapeutic effect. It should be remembered that this hopeless prognosis is not a value judgement, and applies only to the group therapy in question, that is time limited arts therapies. Individuals with this combination of positives and negatives may still be helped by individual therapy and/or a long-term group therapy opportunity.

consensus between co-workers wherever possible, although I have found an earlier version to have strong inter-rater reliability (between 83 and 100 per cent). I would suggest offering a place in the programme to all women except the most hopeless, since if you have got your screening right you will now be left only with those women for whom this therapy is suitable. It is possible that the modality is not suitable, in which case the woman will probably decide for herself not to pursue the opportunity. Careful discussion can almost always allow the individual to make an informed choice. Overall reliability of the earlier version of the checklist in predicting outcome is 78 per cent over a small sample (more information about how this figure was achieved is given in Appendix 2).

COMMUNICATING YOUR DECISION

Once you have made your decision, which should not be a surprise for the client if your discussions have been sensitive but honest throughout, you will need to construct a simple letter to the referrer. This should convey the following information: when you saw the client; what your risk assessment is in relation to the therapy on offer; the goals that your client has chosen to work towards (make sure these are realistic); and the plan (whether or not a place has been offered, and for when). I like to read the letter to the client before having it typed, so that she can make suggestions for amendments if necessary. It is important to discuss the circulation of this letter with your client. For example, whether it will be sent only to the referrer, or to others (psychiatrist, general practitioner).

Recording

All therapy groups need recording systems, and you will need to decide yours in advance. I favour a very simple style of recording sheet, a sample of which is given in Figure 4.8. Each circle on the sheet represents a group member or therapist, with the exception of the central circle, which represents the group process as a whole entity. The top left-hand portion of each person's circle is used to record the check-in and early part of the session, the top right-hand segment being for the end of the session. The bottom half of the circle is left for the main process in the group, including themes that emerge. I then draw lines between the circles to indicate important interactions between people.

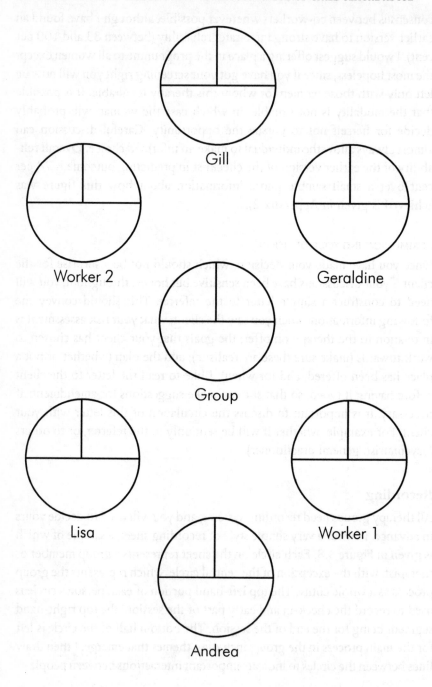

Figure 4.8 – Recording sheet

Summary

In this chapter, I have attempted to help you to set the scene for actually getting started on a group. We began with the importance of adequate supervision, then went on to look at practical issues like location, time and day, number of sessions, number of group members, and how to publicise your group. We continued by looking at co-work preparation, and at safety issues. From there, we moved on to consider clinical issues like the need for eclecticism, a certain therapist style which offers real choice to clients, and the importance of therapeutic boundaries. Having considered such weighty topics, we returned to practical matters, including useful equipment, and how to structure the session. We then examined the assessment process in detail. Finally, we looked at a simple method of recording. You are now almost ready to go, but not before you have read and tried out the techniques described in the following chapters. Good luck!

CHAPTER FIVE

Beginnings

Introduction

It is your first session. If you are feeling nervous, you can assume that the group participants are feeling ten times worse. They will be wondering why they turned up at all. You have at least had the head start of meeting each of them individually for assessment. Moreover, so far as they know, you do not hold the kind of secret which they all hold and are about to disclose implicitly to several new people, simply by turning up to the group. The secret not only will be bound up in painful memories which they would rather ignore if only they could, but also will be associated with shame and the wish to hide. They may be feeling angry with you for even suggesting that they expose themselves in this way.

For these reasons, and a host of others, the first few sessions will be spent on establishing the boundaries of safety in the group, while slowly introducing the working methods which can be called upon in the middle phase of the therapy. In a twenty-session programme, the early phase lasts about four to six sessions.

I am very careful about the use of game structures. Many abusers, as part of their 'grooming' tactics, will have played games with the little girl. Such games may have at first seemed enticing, especially if no other adults were available to give such attention. Games like hide and seek, doctors and nurses, or mummies and daddies, all can be turned to the abuser's advantage and quickly lose their innocent charm. Instead, the little girl may feel guilty and ashamed for having wanted to play, and lose trust in her own ability to suspend disbelief in the way that children do when playing symbolically. She may explain the resulting confusion by saying that she is not creative, or blame the therapist or the activity for making her feel 'stupid'. Certain movement activities, in particular the more creative or expressive structures and use of some hand-held props, should be avoided in this early stage for similar reasons. Hand-held props might remind the survivor of parts of the abuser's body which she may have been forced to touch during the abuse. Expressive movement may make her feel too visible, and too aware of her body.

I will now describe the techniques I use in these early sessions.

Checking in and group discussion

Verbal discussion is likely to be a part of every group session. In Chapter 4, I gave a possible session structure which incorporated the idea of a check-in at the beginning, and a similar period towards the end of the session to process the time spent together.

There are various ways to structure this time. Some women will feel more comfortable with speaking in the group than others, and so you may need some way to help group members to equalise the attention given to each individual. You can check in using a creative structure, for example describing how you feel in terms of weather (I feel like the calm before the storm, I feel like a drizzly day in the garden, etc.) Or, you can suggest that everyone shows the group how they are feeling with a simple movement, possibly while seated in chairs.

If you want to allow for more discussion, you might want to introduce an equivalent of the aboriginal American talking stick. The idea is that whoever has the stick may speak and is heard, without interruptions. The stick is then placed down in the centre of the circle (for example on a small table) and picked up only when another group member feels that they have something important to say. The group facilitators may wish to make a rule that no one can hold the stick twice during any one discussion. The group members may choose a teddy-bear or other object to substitute for the talking stick.

Name games

There are various name games that I use with new groups. One idea, so that group members can check for whether they live near to each other (a source of anxiety for some), is for each woman to say her name and the area in which she lives.

One simple name game is to throw a ball across the circle, calling your own name. When everyone has received the ball a couple of times, this can change to calling the name of the person to whom you are throwing.

Another possible name game involves each person in turn saying: 'Hello, my name is [Janine] and if I were an animal [or car, or piece of food, or plant, etc.] I'd be…'

Once the group members are comfortable with saying their own and each other's names, they can begin to progress to noticing things about each other. This progression is very useful if the person suffers from social anxiety. One of the cognitive processes involved in social anxiety is an overemphasis on how the individual imagines they are perceived. This results in some filtering out of information about others. An antidote to this difficulty would be a name game in which each woman says, 'Hello, Sylvia, I notice that you have red hair' (or whatever is noticed). Eye contact is an important aspect of this structure. An alternative would be to use some other means of contact, for example handing round a talking stick (see the section on group discussion, p.140).

A more advanced name game is for the whole group to keep a rhythm of two claps and two thigh taps of even duration (no gaps). A name is said during the thigh taps, one for each set of two thigh taps. Each woman calls her own name, progressing round the circle. When this has happened twice through, the whole group calls each woman's name in turn.

For groups who are especially interested in movement, it is possible to do a name game which involves each woman saying her name and making a movement for how she is feeling. I should caution here that I have not found that this one works especially well with survivors of CSA who are also new to expressive movement.

One last idea, slightly easier than making an original movement for how you feel, is to give yourself a movement adjective, and perform the movement associated with that adjective. So, for example, I could be 'reaching Bonnie'. When my turn comes I would say these two words and make a reaching movement. The usefulness of this, while not necessarily encouraging authenticity, is that it allows group members to experiment with expressive movement without having to 'own' it.

Making group rules and agreements

In the first session, the group therapists encourage members to set group agreements, with the aid of a flip-chart. The list of agreements made is then typed and copied for each group member. Some rules are set, for example confidentiality, the meaning of which is carefully defined for each woman at assessment (see Chapter 4).

Drawing the end of the rainbow

For this, you will need paper and art materials. Each woman takes a piece of paper and sits with it in front of her. She is then asked to imagine that there is a rainbow. At the end of the rainbow, is her own special future, after recovery from the trauma of child sexual abuse. What does she see at the end of the rainbow? She can then choose materials with which to represent this. Images can be discussed in pairs, before sharing with the whole group. This exercise can be used to examine how realistic the end of the rainbow might be, and what might be needed in order either to realise this vision or to modify it to become more accessible.

The bill of rights

The group are encouraged in either the first or second session, again with the aid of a flip-chart, to examine their goals for therapy and state these as a series of 'rights'. This list is 'brainstormed', that is nothing is censored unless clearly socially unacceptable. For example, it is quite possible for the list to include items such as 'I have the right to dress smartly' together with 'I have the right to dress casually'. But it would not be acceptable to include an item such as 'I have the right to sex with children'. An example of a 'bill of rights' is given in Figure 5.1.

Creating a base camp

The group members are provided with a range of objects, including any furniture in the room, pieces of cloth, symbolic objects, props including balls and so on. From these, they together construct a 'base camp', a safe place to start from on their metaphorical journey into recovery. Afterwards, they discuss the meaning of what they have created.

Provisions for the journey

The group members form a circle around a trunk, real or imagined. They place objects, real or imagined into the trunk, which have symbolic significance for them as provisions for the journey. These might include a map, a compass, a light and some chocolate. Each person's particular contribution is noted and discussed, in terms of their fears and expectations about the journey, and what will be needed in order for them to feel safe.

Figure 5.1
Bill of rights

I have the right to feel safe on the streets

I have the right to feel safe in my bed

I have the right to be special to someone

I have the right to have children

I have the right to define my own sexuality

I have the right to say no

I have the right to get angry

I have the right to be calmer and less angry

I have the right to be heard

I have the right to laughter

I have the right to dance

I have the right to act 'silly' without apologising

I have the right to live rather than just exist

I have the right to make mistakes

I have the right to space for myself

I have the right to be fulfilled

I have the right to feel more whole

I have the right to reclaim my life

Warming up the body

Many survivors feel alienated from their bodies. If they have already accepted that this is so, and decided that they want to do something about this, a gentle wake-up and warm-up activity might be useful. This can initially be left on the level of simple movements that explore the movement of the joints, beginning at the extremities and working progressively through the body over several sessions. It helps to do this with music playing in the background, so that group members are free to respond to the dynamic quality of the music. Initially, the warm-up can be led by the group facilitator, but after a week or two group members may wish to suggest a body part that needs waking up or freeing of tension. Eventually, individual group members may be able to lead the warm-up as in a follow-my-leader structure (see pp.168–169).

Developments from the idea of warming up the joints could be stretching in different directions, shaking limbs, or stroking, patting, rubbing or massaging one's own extremities (e.g. hands).

If you are not a movement specialist, it is important to obtain advice from an expert (e.g. physiotherapist) regarding injury prevention before using movement structures with clients. General guiding principles are to work slowly and gently, avoiding strain on the joints. Advise group members never to do any movement that hurts. Group members should be encouraged to listen to their own bodies, but this is often difficult at first (see the dilemma of embodiment, pp.88–92).

Noticing

One important task in preparing the survivor for disclosure is the reconnection of cognitive processes with sensory information. Without sensory awareness, the survivor will probably disclose in a very detached, dissociated manner, which can be less helpful than not disclosing at all.

I do not suggest that all senses be engaged at this stage. I would suggest starting with the visual and kinaesthetic senses, to aid grounding in present reality. Visual sensory information can be engaged through one of the name games mentioned above. Particularly useful might be the game which requires each group member to tell someone what they notice about them. This is a very useful exercise, as visual awareness of the group will later be very important in helping the survivor to maintain present reality during disclosure.

Another way to take in visual information is for the group members to walk around the room in pairs, taking it in turns within each pair to tell partners what is observed. Each pair of women can then feed back to the whole group about the exercise. Be prepared for the possibility that some of what is seen may at times remind group members of traumatic memories. Even a colour may be restimulating in this way. If this does occur, it may be necessary to reassociate the colour with less emotionally charged memories.

Kinaesthetic information can be linked into the grounding exercise (pp.146–148).

Images of protection

Images of protection can be created individually or collectively, either through modelling (for example with clay or play dough), drawing or painting, choosing a symbolic object, stories and myths which can be told and/or enacted, use of music, or movement. The latter can be explored via the protection warrior dance (see below). Contributions are shared and discussed.

Signature

Each woman is encouraged to write her signature on a piece of paper, then to write it again in the air, as small or as large as she wants to, then to trace it with her feet, as a pathway through the space. It is important to share afterwards in the group, what felt comfortable and what felt uncomfortable, including the implications of this for the individual's sense of her right to take up space or be here.

Protection warrior dance

This activity is included here as it deals with the theme of protection. However, since it makes use of expressive movement it is better placed near to the middle of the programme, and possibly not in the first four sessions. Ultimately, this decision needs to made in response to the process of your particular group. Group members stand in a circle, and each person contributes one movement on the theme of 'protection'. As always, those who do not feel comfortable in contributing a movement are encouraged to stay in the circle if they wish, without pressure to 'perform'. Following each group member's contribution, her movement is mirrored back to her by the group as a whole. All of the movements thus contributed are then combined into a dance, which is performed by the whole group several times in succession, to music chosen by the group. This dance can be returned to in subsequent sessions, as the 'protection warrior dance', or under a different name, again chosen by the group members.

Throwing the ball

This can be a simple and non-threatening way to engage with each other in movement. A foam football, or medium-sized physiotherapy ball, is thrown or kicked around the room. Group members can be encouraged to add sounds or vocalisations to the movement, and can discuss this afterwards.

Happy memories

Any of the art forms can be used here. For example, group members can write about a happy memory, and read or have the story read out to the group. Certain happy memories can be acted out. A piece of music or a song may be associated with a happy memory, and this can be shared with the group. Movement games from childhood may provide other happy memories, although games may be tricky as these are sometimes used by abusers in order to 'groom' children for abuse, as discussed earlier. Childhood stories or poems can be brought to the group sessions, provided that they hold entirely positive associations, as can certain photographs perhaps. Art materials provide an opportunity to represent a happy memory pictorially, thus making it tangible. Lastly, most people are able to respond to the following instruction: rub your hands together, to wake them up. Then, stop and look at them, and tell the group the first positive association that comes to mind, in which your hands were or are significant. Because the hands are important in how we manipulate our environment, and in our close relationships, images of work competencies and of caring behaviours towards children often emerge.

Grounding

Grounding is the name given to the sense that one is rooted in the present, aware of one's source of support. Grounding helps the individual to feel stronger, more powerful and less fragile. This can be achieved in several stages, working through different positions of stillness and movement. The least threatening position is usually seated; both lying down and standing up can make survivors feel vulnerable and evoke memories of the abuse. A lying down position limits one's ability to see whoever might be approaching, and limits one's ability to get away quickly. Standing up may mean that one is more visible and open. So, beginning with a seated position, follow these instructions:

> If it feels comfortable to do so, close your eyes. If this is not possible, I suggest that you allow your eyes to rest on a spot a little way in front of your feet, on the floor. This will help you to concentrate more on what you are feeling. When we feel anxious, we tend to tense up, literally raising the centre of gravity in our bodies as we do so. This makes us less stable, more easily toppled, and we experience this both as a physical reality, and as a metaphorical, emotional reality. In other words, we

literally are a bit more shaky on our feet, and we tend to feel a bit more 'wobbly' emotionally. It takes practise to resist this automatic response to fear and anxiety, but when we do resist it, we often feel more confident and able to cope. The following exercise is designed to help you to resist the automatic response to tighten up, and to get you back in touch with a firm base of support.

The way we are going to do this is to make use of our breathing. The first stage is to use the breath to let go of unnecessary tension. I'm going to take you on a journey through your muscles, suggesting that as we arrive at a spot in your body, you move that area a little, just to increase your awareness of it, then on the out-breath consciously let go of any tension. So, let's begin with the place where your head rests on your spine. It might help if you find this with your fingers – it's roughly mid-way between the tops of your ears – and just as Atlas held up the world, the atlas bone at the top of your spine holds up your skull, on two little rockers. The rocking motion makes the 'yes' movement. It might help to make the tiniest nod you can right now. The next bone down is the axis, and this gives the 'no' movement. So try a tiny one of those. Now, take a decent breath in, and let it right out, releasing all unnecessary tension in your neck.

Linked to your neck is your jaw. We hold a lot of tension in our jaws, particularly related to anxiety and unexpressed anger. Feel that place where your jaws meet, right up near your ears again. If it helps, massage this a little, then let go with the out-breath so that your teeth are a little way apart, even when your mouth is closed.

Moving on to your shoulders, give them some gentle movement, then let go again on the out-breath. Now check that you are not holding in at the waist, and hips…each time, letting go on the out breath.

Now, focus on your hands, wrists and arms. It's surprising how much tension is held in these areas. Move, and let go.

Move back to your hips, and down to your legs, particularly the tops of your legs. Move a little, and let go. Finally, your feet. Let them spread out on the floor, wiggle your toes, and let go.

Now that you are relaxed, you are ready to focus more on the ground, and on the chair. Notice which bits of you are in contact with these surfaces. Without either resisting the contact or pressing into the chair or the floor, can you allow yourself to be even more supported?

Suspending disbelief for a while, because the next bit is only an image and not really what happens, imagine that you can breathe through your feet! As you breathe in, imagine you can take in energy from the centre of the earth, bringing this up into a point just below your navel. Now, as you breathe out, imagine that you can send this energy throughout your body, right to your skin, up into your head, down your arms, and of course back down your legs as well. If at any time you find yourself feeling light headed, just concentrate on bringing the energy up as far as your navel, then back down again. Your breathing should be quiet and easy, not noisy or too deep, just relaxed.

Now, begin to bring your attention back to your position in the room, stretch a little, and slowly open your eyes if they are closed, but leave them resting on the spot in front of you on the floor for a while, before raising them to face the circle.

A development of the sitting grounding exercise is to do this while standing, a little more quickly perhaps, and then to take a slow walk around the room, concentrating on each step taken, and on the transfer of weight from one leg to the other. A 'Tai Chi Walk' is especially good for grounding (see standing your ground and moving forward, pp.170–171). For this, you have the knees slightly bent and soft, and you imagine that when standing on both legs each of them is half full with a fluid. As the weight transfers to just one leg, this one becomes full and the other empties. Only when the leg is completely empty does the foot peel off the floor and become placed down in a new position. Once on the floor, the transfer of weight can begin, and the fluid slowly transfers. The balance comes from imagining that this transfer happens through a point just below the navel. This point is known in Japanese martial arts as the 'Hara', in Tai Chi as the 'Tan Tien', and is a centre for power and balance roughly corresponding to the centre of gravity in the body. Once the slow walk is mastered, transfers of weight which are more quickly executed can be practised, perhaps through a short movement improvisation.

Circle dance

There are many circle dances, and classes are available in most areas for you to learn. For your GAT-P, it is best to choose one or two dances, with very simple steps and an even, gentle rhythm. I favour a Greek circle dance called 'Menoussis', in which the group members move towards and away from the centre of the circle, with a slow progression anti-clockwise in the space. This can be used at the end of sessions, becoming a marker for the ending of the session. It is also a way to reaffirm group identity.

Those group facilitators who are unfamiliar with circle dance can use any piece of gentle, regularly rhythmic music. A simple sequence of steps can be developed and taught, while the group members hold hands or hankies to join them together. The important thing here is that the facilitator feels comfortable with the medium of movement, and has worked out the steps in advance. These can be as simple as step to the side and close four times, followed by four slow steps in to the centre and four out, then whatever is needed to complete the musical phrase. The completion may, for example, be a side step in the other direction, although it is useful if there is some progression round the circle overall, to give the sense that one is not 'getting nowhere'. Different rhythms in the music will require different numbers of steps.

Guided imagery: the garden

Some of the women I have worked with have found this exercise particularly useful. One of my clients referred to it as her 'secret garden'. With all guided visualisations, I begin with a short relaxation similar to that used at the beginning of the grounding exercise above. I then proceed like this:

> Imagine yourself in a very beautiful garden, which is all yours. You are the only person in this garden, which has a high, strong fence or wall surrounding it, and a sturdy gate. The gate is locked, and you hold the key close to your body. Take some time to walk around this garden – how big is it? What do you find in there – plants, animals, birds, butterflies? Have only the things that feel good to you in there – anything else, you can remove or have removed in whatever way you choose. Notice what the weather is like, what you are wearing, and how the garden is arranged, with generous garden furniture, lawns, flower beds, ponds – whatever you want.

> Now, imagine that someone of your choosing, with whom you would like to share this garden for a short while, is waiting patiently outside the gate. If you choose, and only if you choose, go to the gate and unlock it. Let only one person in, the one you want. Be sure to lock the gate behind the person you have let in. Now, if it feels right, spend a bit of time with this person. Notice what happens…now, escort the person to the gate,

say goodbye, watch as the person exits, and lock the gate again after-wards. Now, go back to enjoying your garden all alone, in full confidence that you can share it with whomever you choose, whenever you choose. You are in total control.

A safe place in the room

It may be useful to have a clear demarcation in the room between the areas for action and reflection. The ideal studio is divided into two sections; approximately two-thirds is covered with linoleum and used for the 'active' part of the session, where either movement or visual art structures are employed. The other third is carpeted, and a circle of chairs is arranged in this area. This becomes the 'talking' area. The movement between sections of the room becomes symbolic of engaging different aspects of the group members' psyches. In general, the 'active' space is often associated with regression to childhood (the activities being conducted at a lower level and using creative, often non-verbal media). The 'talking' section engages more adult defences (such as verbalisation and sitting in chairs) and thus helps individuals to feel 'put back together' before leaving the session.

It might be useful to suggest, as a piece of creative work, that each woman moves around the studio, trying out different areas and levels, to see how they each feel. Where does she feel safe, and why? Then discuss this as a group.

Developing group empathy through movement

There are many ways to develop group empathy, not least the 'witnessing' of each other's creative and verbal contributions. Shared rhythms and mirrored or reciprocal body movements echo early good-enough mother–child inter-action, and thus enable each person to feel they belong (Meekums 1990). One simple structure for developing this, once the group members have become familiar with the medium of structured movement, is 'follow-my-leader'. It might help group members if a task is given, such as focusing on movement of hands or feet. If this is too difficult for some group members initially, I suggest using a prop. The whole group can move together, holding onto either a piece of stretch lycra cloth or a circle of wide elastic.

Once the structure of 'follow-my-leader' is mastered first with, then without a prop, it might be possible to set up movement in pairs. For some people, this can be too confronting, and so choice is paramount as usual. The most difficult version of a pair dance would be to move with some part of the body in contact, for example the hands. One way to make the task less confronting is to suggest a side to side position rather than facing, while holding onto a garden stick or a scarf, which necessitates that a certain distance is maintained. The cautions given in the introduction regarding props and expressive movement should be borne in mind when deciding whether or not to use these ideas. As always, be guided by your group, and be ready with several alternatives.

The sun shines on

This is a game structure, and as such should be used with care. It is important to discuss first whether the playing of games might present any difficulties for anyone, describe the game, and allow group members to choose whether or not to participate.

Each woman, including one of the two therapists, chooses an object which is large enough to stand behind (e.g. a handbag or shoe) and places it on the floor in the room. She then stands behind her object. The second therapist stands out, and declares, 'The sun shines on all those who...', finishing the sentence with some statement which is true of herself. The statement can be obvious and not very self-revealing, for example '...have brown hair'. On the other hand, it can be slightly more personal, for example '...feel upset when they watch the news about children who are suffering'. The therapists can model the move from no self-disclosure to appropriate self-disclosure during the course of the game.

Once the group members have heard the declaration, they move from their spot if the statement is also true for them. Their task is then to find another spot to occupy. They cannot return to their own spot until another statement has been made. The 'odd one out' is also competing for a spot, and inevitably someone will be left out again. It is then that person's turn to make a statement to the group.

I find it helpful if the first go is labelled a 'trial run', to reduce anxiety. Eventually, the game can be a source of much hilarity.

Swimming pool

This exercise is borrowed from psychodrama. Group members are asked if they would like to place themselves in the room as if in part of a swimming pool complex. Areas are defined in advance, including deep and shallow ends, diving board, pool edges, cafeteria, changing rooms and so on. The group therapists then suggest that each woman speaks about where she has chosen to place herself, what she imagines she might be wearing, what she is doing and thinking in that position, whether it feels comfortable or not and so on. She is then invited to reflect on this choice in relation to her involvement in the group, and to her recovery process.

The exercise can be repeated, with a different instruction: each participant is asked to place herself in the swimming pool as she would like to be by the end of the programme. Each woman is then invited to reflect on this choice, and on what might need to happen before she can arrive at that point in her recovery. The information obtained from this exercise can be used to enhance assessment, and if it is repeated towards the end of the programme it can provide evidence of change.

One caution: this exercise should not be attempted until group members have developed some ease with self-disclosure.

Goodbye

I find it extremely helpful if the group can find a way to end each session, which can be repeated each week. This helps each woman to mark the ending psychologically, leaving behind the content of the session. I do find that most groups in mental health settings have difficulty in choosing an ending, unless I present some options to them. Some of the most successful endings I have found are the protection warrior dance; a simple circle dance to music, for example 'Menoussis'; standing in a circle holding hands (if members of the group can tolerate this level of contact), thinking about the connection and support in the group and about each woman's grounding in the earth; sitting in a circle, and saying one word for how you have experienced today's session; sitting in a circle, and saying one word for how you feel now; and symbolically giving yourself a gift to take away from the session, for example a promise to listen to some nice music in the week.

Summary

In this chapter, we looked at some of the structures you can use in the first few sessions with a group of women who have survived the experience of CSA. I have been cautious in emphasising those structures that are most likely to allow the women to build a sense of safety and strength in the group, at the same time as building empathic relationships. There are many more options you can try, from your own repertoire and creativity. Whatever you do, always bear in mind the context in which you are working, and the individual's right to choose.

CHAPTER SIX

The Middle Phase

Introduction

Once the group is functioning with a certain level of trust and self-disclosure, it is time to move on to the phase in the programme that deals more directly with the issue of CSA. The middle phase of the programme is likely to be the longest, spanning approximately sessions five to sixteen in a twenty-session programme. Many of the techniques discussed in Chapter 5 will also be relevant here, in order to reinforce basic security, but the main focus will be disclosure about the abuse. It is more important than ever to bear in mind each woman's right to determine the extent to which she engages with any of the activities suggested here, and the amount of detail in any disclosure. Disclosure is essentially about telling one's story. A story has a beginning, a middle and an end, and as such provides a containing structure which includes the point at which the individual survives the experience. This is a very important part of the story, and should not be ignored. Even if the ending is not overt in the telling, it is helpful if therapists make reference to the implied ending to the story, namely survival. One other important concept relevant to disclosure is Elsa Jones' notion of the 'relevant account' (Jones 1991). Therapists may be tempted to suggest that more should be told, but survivors must be encouraged to tell their own story, which is bound to be an abridged version of events. It may not be necessary to reveal in detail the nature of the abuse. Far more important than such details, is the meaning that the survivor attributes to the experience, for it is this that determines her response to life events.

There is general agreement that the telling of the story is useful to recovery only if the survivor makes some connection with affect during the telling, balanced by an awareness of present reality. It is not generally helpful to encourage a complete regression or 'reliving' of the experience, to the extent that the survivor forgets how old she is now, where she is and so on.

There is also general agreement (Hackman 1999; Parks 1990) that it helps if the story is not left at disclosure of the awfulness of it all. A careful reworking of the story may enable the survivor to feel differently about events, and attach new meaning to them. Generally, this involves a symbolic rescuing of the 'inner child', perhaps by the survivor's 'adult self' or by the group as a whole, while acknowledging the fact that this did not happen in historical reality.

A word about anger. It is often at this stage in the group process that anger emerges as a theme. However, extreme displays of anger can feel very frightening for some women. I have to say that I have not found the classic exercise of bashing cushions in order to 'cathart' to be very helpful in achieving a resolution for angry feelings. In fact, far from being cathartic in the true sense, the exercise often generates more arousal, and does nothing to assist a person who fears loss of control. Alternative strategies, which address the need for containment of feelings via metaphor, might include for example image-making on paper, followed by some fine motor involvement with that paper, rather than whole body movement in a large space. I remember one woman who, recalling that her mother had claimed not to have seen the abuse her daughter was suffering, painted a picture of her mother, then put out the eyes with a paintbrush. Another woman painted an image which represented the abuse, then tore up the image. A third placed a puppet which represented the abuser in a small plastic dustbin, and threw the dustbin down some stairs outside the studio.

Checking in and group discussion

This continues to be a very important part of each session. It is probable that, as group members become more at ease with each other, they will reveal more about themselves. It is important to find a balance between allowing enough time for group members to say what is essential, while not sacrificing the creative work which will be a vehicle for disclosure, containment and transformation. Remember to make good use of structures which assist focused discussion, including 'talking sticks' and the like (see Chapter 5). The notion of allowing each woman to speak and be heard without interruption is crucial in each of the exercises which follow.

Keeping safe (1)

One useful movement exercise at this stage is to provide the group with a variety of large cloths (saris are ideal), which can be used by each woman to wrap around her body while gentle music plays. The process can be assisted by words of encouragement from the group therapists, to suggest that each woman can use the cloth to enable her to feel safe. At the same time, she is encouraged to consider how this links to her survival strategies over the years. I suggest that, when the time comes to talk about this experience, each woman is given the option of either continuing to 'wear' the cloth or discarding it. Bearing in mind that survival strategies such as hiding in cupboards or under beds may have been ineffectual in avoiding the abuse, this exercise may be too confronting for some women. If this is the case, they should be encouraged to find a different way to feel safe. For those who are able to make use of the cloth to develop feelings of safety, it can be suggested that they might wish to use the same piece of cloth each week during any disclosure work.

Keeping safe (2)

A second way to establish a safe place symbolically in the room is to suggest that each woman places objects around her, like a 'magic circle'. These might include drawings or photographs of loved ones who were or are now protective (obviously some preparation needs to go into this over one or two sessions), musical instruments including drums to beat so that the alarm can be raised, mythical figures and so on. Again, some gentle music can be played while the survivor arranges her safe place and enters this. Each group member is then encouraged to talk about her safe place, and before leaving it she is asked whether she is able to internalise an image of this that she can keep with her during the disclosure work.

Sculpting

In this exercise, each woman is asked to make a sculpt of her family of origin and of her present family. Various symbols can be used to make this sculpt, including small figures, puppets, soft toys, cushions or drawings. I have even been known to use pens in the absence of my usual props. One object is used to represent each member of the family or wider system. This might include babysitters, friends of the family, and people who were not alive during the survivor's childhood but who still were 'present' in the family's hearts and minds. The objects are then arranged in a way that denotes their relationship to each other. The sculpts can be discussed within the wider group.

Life map

Each group member is encouraged to create a 'life map', from birth or pre-birth to the present day, and beyond. In a group situation, this is best done using art materials. The map may be very simple, using a straight line, or it may be far more complex, making use of symbolism in the way the map is constructed in order to represent key events. Each map can then be discussed in the group.

How I survived

Prior to disclosure of the 'story' of the abuse, it may be useful for group members to share with each other the ways that they have survived over the years. This can help to explain their present symptoms (for example dissociation) and contribute to the sense of shared experience. There are various ways to do this, the most obvious one being group discussion. However, it may help to draw or write about the experience. In order to begin to understand projectively how the little girl's body reacted at the time of abuse, a manikin can be manipulated to show body postures and talk about how each one feels. A further alternative is to brainstorm as a group the ways in which each little girl survived, and to flip-chart these contributions. Lastly, some women may prefer to draw an image of how they survived. Whatever method is used, time must be set aside to discuss what has been created.

Containers

This exercise is a projective way of addressing the need for containment in the telling of the story, and as such provides a level of safety. A box of containers is placed in the centre of the circle, on a small table. Such containers might include, for example, a wooden chest; a miniature chest of cardboard drawers used for writing paper; a glass bottle with stopper; trinket boxes and so on. Each woman chooses a container that she feels is suitable to contain her 'story'. She then writes, in coloured felt-tip, one to three words on each of three index cards or pieces of paper. Each of these headings represents an important part of her story, which she feels she might be able to share with the group. The headings might include names of abusers, or aspects of the abuse and its effects. She places the cards or pieces of paper in her container. The women then take turns to share whatever they want with the group about the container and its contents. One disadvantage of this method is that the containers and their contents should ideally remain available to the group members from week to week, until they are dealt with. An alternative might be to provide envelopes and sticky tape, asking the women to imagine what kind of container their envelope represents.

Myths and stories

There are various myths and stories that can be used to enable the survivor to connect with the experience of abuse in its archetypal form. Work with archetypes is a useful way both to provide some emotional distance from the experience, and to enable the survivor to sense the fact that she is not the only one who has ever felt as she does. One such myth is that of the rape and abduction of Persephone. Another is that of Red Riding Hood, or perhaps the Babes in the Woods. It might be useful to have a range of stories to hand, covering various cultures. The story can be read to the group, and responses aired. An interim step might be to encourage some image-making from the story, whether using art materials solely or perhaps using collage materials including images from women's magazines perhaps. A combination of words and images might empower the survivor to express her response to the story. One important aspect of working with stories is that they can be rewritten. Rewriting might include the use of the group as a powerful force in overcoming the perpetrator. This can then be acted out, using either each woman in turn as the person to be rescued, or using a symbolic object like a cushion, doll or puppet.

Symbolic objects

Each woman chooses an object from the box of symbolic objects. The box contains various items that can be imbued with significance. These might include a small bread roll in the shape of a loaf, a candle, a piece of chain, a key, a toy knife, toy furniture including a bed, a wardrobe and a bath, small containers, means of transport including ambulances, police cars, planes, cars and helicopters, masks, and a teddy-bear. She then uses this object, to assist her in telling part of her story to the group.

Childhood image

Each woman chooses art materials from a range, including paints, oil pastels, charcoal, chalk and various colours of paper in large sizes. She then makes an image of her childhood, and uses this to disclose part of her story to the group. In later sessions, an image of hope may be added, but only after the image has been used to demonstrate to the survivor how helpless she was at the time. This is important, in order to enable her to locate responsibility for her suffering outside herself. The image of hope may be used to enable the adult woman now to rescue her 'inner child', so that she can begin to parent herself. In discussing images, each woman is encouraged to speak first about the image she has created, before choosing whether to invite feedback from others. Feedback is non-judgemental, and all perceptions owned by the perceiver rather than offered as absolute truth.

Photographs

Those women who wish, and are ready to do so, may want to bring photographs of children into the group, for discussion. It might be best to begin with children unknown to the group members, for example images in magazines, progressing to images of oneself or one's family. The discussion that ensues can serve to enable the survivor to face the reality that she was small and defenceless against an adult, at the time of the abuse. This is an important step in releasing herself from guilt and blame, and placing this with the abuser. However, it is inevitably a distressing step to pass through, and must be approached with caution. Some women do not need to bring photographs of themselves, but benefit by witnessing the photographs of others.

Drawing the cause

Each woman chooses from a range of art materials, then creates an image of the cause for her anger and/or grief. She can then physically engage with the image, for example by tearing it up, stamping on it and putting it in the bin. It may be possible, if safe incineration is available, to burn the image. However, health and safety rules must come before any potentially therapeutic effects; sometimes it is enough to imagine it burning, if this is what is needed.

It is also possible, once an image of the abuse has been created, to consider what else might have been in the picture. For example, a protector (e.g. a grandmother who died before the abuse occurred) can be brought into the picture, leading to modifications. This may prompt the survivor to create a new image, perhaps of the abuser being placed behind bars. The importance of such image modification lies not in any distortion of actual events, but in a new attribution of meaning. The survivor may for example develop new views about herself in relation to others, leading to increased self-efficacy.

Poems

Group members may wish to bring poems into the group sessions, to share with other group members. These may be written by other survivors, or created by the woman herself. Several of the women I have known through this work have used poetry as a way to organise their thoughts and contain their feelings, at the same time providing a way to communicate their experience. My own clinical experience is that the poem works most powerfully when read by someone other than the woman who has brought it to the group. This enables the woman to witness her own words (or those she needs to empathise with) and to take in the witness of the group. When someone other than the survivor reads her contribution, she is released from 'performing', so that she can fully engage with the experience.

The charge sheet

The charge sheet is a technique used in psychodrama. The idea is, that a proforma (Figure 6.1) is completed by each woman in the group, detailing the abuse and its effects, as evidence in a symbolic 'trial' of the abuser. This trial is then acted out, with the survivor as protagonist. One of the group therapists stands close to the protagonist, encouraging her and perhaps reading out the charge. The rest of the group members play the jury. The same proforma can be used to sentence the abuser in a way that can be incorporated into the trial scene. The punishment is then meted out symbolically by the survivor together with anyone else from the group whom she chooses to assist her. When this works well, many survivors have told me that it was the turning point in their recovery. However, it is crucial that no one is made to feel that they must take part. To whatever extent the survivor can complete any of the proforma, this must be confirmed as a valid decision at this stage in the survivor's recovery. The effects of the trial and punishment on the 'jury' must also be processed, in good time before the ending of the session. This may mean that therapists give active permission for group members to say if they felt uncomfortable. To a large extent, such adverse reactions can be

Figure 6.1 – Charge sheet

I am .... (survivor)

I charge .... with abusing me.

The accused took advantage of their greater power as
.... (relationship to the survivor, e.g. father, school
teacher, babysitter, trusted adult)

The accused abused me from the age of .... to ....,

at/in .... (place)

This is my story of how the accused abused me:

Since then, the abuse has affected my life in the following ways:

The abuser is entirely responsible for his/her own actions, and is therefore
found guilty. He/she will be punished in the following ways:

Once the sentence is carried out, I need to do the following, in order to
reclaim my life:

avoided through a reminder by the therapists at the outset, that each group member can participate to the extent that they feel comfortable. Discussion of coping strategies for both protagonist and auxiliaries (the rest of the group) should precede the event. If each group member is to complete the process, this will take several sessions. If you intend to use this structure, be prepared for it to take up a large chunk of the middle phase of therapy. I would advise anyone thinking of using this structure to consult a qualified psychodramatist first.

Lullaby

The whole group constructs words to go to the tune of Brahms' *Lullaby*, as if they were singing a lullaby to their 'inner child'. Following its construction, the group sings the lullaby together a few times, then each woman takes up a position in the room. From this position, she sings the song to her 'inner child', rocking and comforting her. Floor cushions, large pieces of cloth, soft toys and baby dolls may all be used as symbolic representations of the 'inner child'. A tape of the music may be useful. The lullaby is sung several times. Group members are encouraged to picture their 'inner child' being loved and protected. Singing can be as quiet or as loud as each woman wishes. I suggest that the group therapists sing along, as a way of 'holding the space' and witnessing the process.

Letters

These are letters that will never be sent. Some survivors find it difficult to see the point in writing such a letter at first, but if they are able to suspend disbelief the experience can be genuinely cathartic, and may lead to shifts in self-perception in relation to the abuse. It is often useful to provide plain paper and coloured felt-tips so that the individual can choose which colour to use, and what size to write in. Examples of letters might be from the 'inner child' to the abuser; from the 'inner child' to an adult who might have been trustworthy, had they been available at the time, or if the survivor had been able to disclose to them as a child (survivors often choose to write to a dead grandparent, for example); from the 'inner child' to a non-protecting adult; from the 'inner child' to the adult self; to the 'inner child' from the adult self (see Parks 1990); to the 'inner child' from a trustable adult. Sometimes the sequence in which these letters are written is important. For example, it is logical to write the letter from the 'inner child' to the trustable adult prior to an answer. It is often helpful for these letters to be read aloud by one of the group therapists, provided that the group member wishes this. In hearing her own words witnessed in his way, the survivor is able to empathise more fully with her 'inner child', and to allow herself to experience any associated feelings.

Laying to rest

Sometimes, group members bring issues of real losses through death. There may also be a need to mourn the loss of one's own childhood. Sometimes it is helpful for the group to construct a respectful ceremony, in order to say goodbye. For example, in one of the groups I co-facilitated, a woman needed to mourn her dead baby. The session in which we were to do this was carefully planned in advance, and on the day several women brought flowers and other objects to support the process. A baby doll was chosen by the woman concerned, to represent her lost loved one. One therapist stood by her side, and the other therapist positioned herself with the other group members, forming a circle. The grieving woman took her baby to each of the women in the circle, all of whom chose to hold it and say a few words. After this, the baby was wrapped in a cloth and laid on a cushion, together with flowers and other tributes. The group finally chose to dance the circle dance 'Menoussis', which had been used at the end of each session to mark our goodbye.

Closing the session

Effective closure of sessions becomes even more crucial at this stage in the therapy. A clear closure, with enough time to mark the ending, allows group members to 'switch gear' before entering the world outside, and provides an important cognitive and emotional distance from potentially distressing material. This is why it is important to use the early phase of the programme to establish a ceremonial way to close each session. I avoid calling this a closing 'ritual', due to associations with ritualistic abuse. Once a routine way of closing is established, continue to use it as a symbolic link with the safety established in early sessions.

Summary

This chapter has addressed the middle phase of the programme, during which it could be said the core of the therapy takes place. Emotions often run high; the material dealt with in sessions is often very moving for therapists and group members alike. For this reason, the safety established in the early sessions and discussed in Chapter 5 is crucial. Ongoing supervision forms part of this strategy. Once you and the group members have survived this part of the programme together, you will have symbolically connected to the survival of the abuse, and be ready to look forward to closure.

CHAPTER SEVEN

Endings

Introduction

The final few sessions (approximately sessions seventeen to twenty in a twenty-session programme) are an important time for any group. For women who have struggled together to break the silence of abuse, this means the opportunity to leave behind the pain of disclosure, and to begin to look forward. It is also a time when boundaries become reaffirmed, redrawn and re-evaluated. For many women, there will be a sense of relief tinged with sadness. Some may feel unable to face the ending, never before having had the opportunity to engage with endings in a way that acknowledges their own feelings. Some may simply stop attending the group. But for those who are able to see it through, the whole process may be very healing. Some important friendships are forged from group therapy. Telephone numbers and addresses may be swapped, promises made to meet without the group therapists, and so on. This can be a tricky time for those who feel ambivalent about the possibility of continued contact. There may be a mixture of feelings, ranging from disbelief that anyone could want to keep in touch with them, to guilt at the real possibility that they may want to leave behind friendships forged from a common identity as abuse survivors. It may be difficult for individuals to voice this ambivalence, and so it is the job of the group therapists to raise the issues as possibilities. This would leave open the possibility for each woman to opt out of future contact and, it is hoped, enable those women whose approaches are rejected to understand that such rejection may not be personal.

Before you read the following exercises, I suggest that you reread the ideas in the previous two chapters, particularly Chapter 5. Many of the early, containing structures are again relevant at this stage in the life of a group. To repeat them can in itself have a containing function, like the closing of a circle. Repetition at this stage also offers the opportunity to reflect on how different the exercises feel now, and thus how far each woman has journeyed. The swimming pool exercise provides a specific way of evaluating this. In the following suggestions, I offer developments for some of these early exercises, as well as new activities which are particularly relevant to the last stage of the programme.

Movement exercises

It may be possible for women to contemplate movement exercises in this part of the group programme, whether or not they have felt able to do so in earlier sessions. This development is made possible by the disassociation of movement from the theme of abuse, and the new association with empowerment and assertion. It is best to start all movement exercises in the safety of the circle, generating ideas for how to respond to the task, before encouraging movement away from the circle. Useful progressions in enabling group members to become easy with movement are circle dances with set steps; movements generated in a circle from group members' ideas (as in the protection warrior dance, see p.145); movement outside of the circle on a given theme.

A movement for how I feel

This is likely to stay at the level of gesture initially, and may never reach the point at which whole body involvement becomes comfortable. However, as a warm-up structure this exercise can be very useful in enabling group members to engage in a brief introduction to the link between affect to movement. As with most of the movement structures proposed here, the process occurs in a circle. Each woman then takes it in turn to contribute a movement for how she is feeling, and the group mirrors this back to her.

Follow my leader

This is a development of the exercise I called developing group empathy through movement (pp.150–151). I suggest you reread that section, to make your own synthesis of the material.

Eventually, it may be possible for the group to begin to move together in a flowing and rhythmic manner. The movement should be led initially by one of the therapists, to music chosen by the group from the range available (remember that group members can offer to bring their own music into sessions, if the whole group agrees to try this). Eventually, through modelling by the therapist, it may be possible to change the movement slightly and gradually; for example, an arm swing may develop to include a finger click. The therapist should make these changes explicit. Then, the therapist can invite the group as a whole to take over leadership, so that anyone can make quite minor changes. Often, these changes will be unconscious, but the therapist can pick these up and amplify them for the group, naming the 'choreographer'. If the group becomes really comfortable with this, a follow-my-leader structure that involves conscious passing of the leadership may be useful, but this is not essential.

The benefits of being able to move in a group together in this way may not be immediately obvious to group members, and should be attempted only when the group therapists are very comfortable with facilitating movement activities. Those groups that do find themselves able to move empathically together will almost certainly find that it facilitates group cohesion. There is likely to be a spin-off for the individual, that in having her own movement mirrored by the group she begins to feel more valued. One of the biggest challenges for some survivors of CSA, however, is often in trusting one's own body cues. It may be paralysing to be faced with the option of moving expressively. If the process is rushed, it can be counter-therapeutic, possibly leading to increased anxieties about being seen in an invasive way, and about the pressure to 'get it right'. If the process is successful, the survivor may just begin to love and trust her body again.

Once expressive movement in the group is mastered, it may also be possible to progress to some examination of the symbolic content in the movement, but again this should not be rushed. The protection warrior dance is an example of a controlled symbolic use of movement, the theme being set in advance.

Rhythm circle

The group sits in a circle, for example on floor cushions. A box of percussion instruments is placed in the centre, and each woman chooses one instrument to play. This might include, for example, wooden blocks, simple shakers made from yoghurt pots with beans inside, drums made from old coffee tins with plastic lids on, or professional instruments if the budget allows. One woman (usually a group facilitator to start with) begins the rhythm circle, by setting a simple, repeated rhythm. Each woman then joins in when she is ready, with a rhythm of her own that may or may not fit in with the first. The facilitator can suggest at various times that the volume increases, decreases, and that the music ceases altogether, using whatever verbal or nonverbal means is readily understood. Afterwards, the group can discuss what it felt like to do this exercise. A variation would be to use body parts and the floor only, to make a sound, or to use voices.

Standing your ground and moving forward

This is best done with each woman in her own space in the room, rather than in a circle formation. Some of the ideas are borrowed from Tai Chi Chuan. You might like to reread the section in Chapter 5 on grounding, to make your own synthesis of this material.

The facilitator says something like this:

> I suggest that you shut your eyes if this is comfortable. Or, if you prefer, you could glance downwards, bringing your attention inwards to what is going on inside your own body. I am going to take you through a visualisation that will help you to feel that you are able to stand your ground. First, become aware of your breathing, the gentle movement of your breath in and out of your body. Have your feet about shoulder width apart and allow your knees to soften, so that they are not rigid or locked. Now, imagine that you could draw energy up from the centre of the earth on each in-breath, as if you had roots that go very deep. Collect this energy in your belly, and on the out-breath send it out along your limbs and into your head, then right out to your skin in all areas. You might want to imagine a particular colour to this energy, one which you feel you need at this time.

> The next stage will be to be able to move from the spot, without losing this sense of solidity. Don't move yet. Imagine that, when you are standing completely on both legs, they are each half full of water. Now, slowly allow the weight to transfer from one leg, and as you do so imagine the water pouring out of this leg and into the other one. Once the weight is completely transferred to the second leg, you can peel the foot off the floor, allow it to move forward, then place it down again, beginning the process of weight transfer all over again and picturing the water pouring from the full leg to the empty leg.

> Now, as you move forward with awareness, notice how this is different from the way you usually move. How does it feel to be moving with this level of awareness and control? Are you aware of where you might be

going? What is possible now that wasn't possible before? How can you use this experience in your daily life? Now, come to stillness and feel that sense of being rooted into the earth again. When you feel ready, find a partner and discuss with her what you have just experienced.

A different kind of strength

This exercise is borrowed from Aikido. Group members form pairs, standing opposite each other. They decide who is going to be 'A', and who 'B'. 'A' places her right arm out at right angles in front of her, using muscular force to try to keep it straight. 'B' tries to bend the arm, by placing pressure on the crook of the elbow, the fingers of her own hands interlocking. Once the arm is bent, or when 'A' or 'B' wishes to stop, the exercise is repeated with the other arm.

In the second phase of the exercise, 'A' takes up a posture similar to the one described in the section on standing your ground (p.170). With soft knees, she becomes aware of energy accumulating in the belly on the in-breath, being sent through the body on the out-breath. The arm is placed quite softly at right angles to the torso, not rigidly straight. At the same time, 'A' visualises that the energy from the belly provides a gush of water along the arm. As with water in a hose pipe, this exerts tremendous pressure to keep the arm supported. When 'A' is ready with her visualisation, she nods to 'B'. She avoids all eye contact and speech, concentrating only on the visualisation. 'B' then applies pressure as before. The exercise is repeated with the other arm.

The pair then discuss the differences between the two sides of the body, and between the rigid arm and the more subtle kind of strength. Most people find that the more subtle form of strength, which makes use of what Japanese martial arts experts call 'ki', is actually stronger than brute strength. This softer kind of strength is easier to locate on the left side of the body if you are right-handed, and vice versa. This general rule tends to hold true in my experience, whatever the gender. The message for women, though, is quite clear: you do not need strong muscles to be strong.

No longer a push over

This exercise also makes use of the 'standing your ground' posture, in pairs. The two face each other again, this time with palms touching or with garden canes between the palms if direct contact feels too threatening. The idea is to maintain an even pressure between the hands throughout the exercise as far as possible. The feet are placed one in front of the other, with a wide base of support, and the knees slightly bent. The spine is visualised as making one long line, so that the upper and lower torso act as one unit rather than breaking at the waist. Now, the pair try very small movements forwards and backwards, maintaining even pressure. This is often quite difficult, and may need some demonstration, so be sure you have tried it first (this goes for all of the activities)! Discussion in pairs may yield some fruitful ideas. Feedback can then be linked in the larger group to the potential metaphors inherent in leaning heavily, holding back, fear of falling, breaking into two, and so on. Once mastered, the exercise gives a strong sense of maintaining one's integrity in a relationship.

Stop!

In this exercise, group members work in pairs. One of the pair faces the other from some distance, then slowly approaches in a straight line. At the point that the woman who is stationary wants the other woman to stop, she extends her arm, palm turned out towards the woman approaching, and says firmly, 'STOP!' The woman who has been moving then stands still. The roles reverse, then each pair discusses what it felt like to be approached and to approach, and how it felt to be in charge. The pairs can then feed back to the whole group.

Room to breathe

This exercise is about reclaiming personal space. Each woman stands in a place of her choosing in the room, feet about shoulder width apart. She then extends her arms out to the side, and slowly rotates in the torso, to check that she has enough space to do so without knocking either into someone else, or into furniture, walls, etc. If she does make contact, she is invited to shift her position slightly until satisfied that she has enough space.

Next, all of the women are invited to place their hands on the front of their torso, at the level of the diaphragm. The diaphragm is a roughly circular sheet of muscle that separates the chest and abdomen. It attaches at the front of the body to the base of the sternum (breast bone) and to the bottom ribs. At the back, it attaches to the ribs and spine. I usually find that the best place to put my own hands is with the fingers lightly touching, just below the breast bone, and the palms of my hands in contact with my ribs. It is then possible to feel the movement of the breath, which should gently push the fingers apart on the in-breath, allowing them to sink back towards each other on the out-breath. The breathing should be soft and noiseless. There should be a sense of no effort, and a joy in filling the lungs as fully, slowly and easily as possible. In order to get a sense of the lungs filling in all directions, I then suggest placing the hands on the ribs at each side, and finally at the back on the ribs. Some people are quite amazed when they realise that they can feel their lungs moving at the back! I also suggest that each woman try to sense internally the effects of the diaphragm moving downwards on the in-breath, pushing out the belly and even subtly causing the pelvic floor to expand. The pelvic floor is the figure of eight of muscle that surrounds the anus and vagina. To get a sense of the front part of this muscle, you can tighten as if stopping yourself from peeing. It is not a good idea to practise this in the middle of a pee, as it causes some back pressure on the kidneys, but it is fine to do at other times and is in fact a useful exercise in prolapse prevention.

The next part of the exercise involves a little movement. I suggest that some gentle, flowing music is used at this point. The movement of the breath is one of opening and closing, expanding and contracting. Each woman is encouraged to sense this movement, allowing it to extend into the arms and spine, making the movement as small or large as she wishes. Each opening movement can occur in a different place in space, so that the survivor literally claims the room around her body, which is her room to breathe. It might be necessary for the group to 'brainstorm' some of the possible directions together first, before encouraging each woman to improvise. Possibilities for directions in which to open include to the side; to front and back with a gentle spinal twist; above the head; one arm up, the other down.

Yes and no

This is an exercise in assertion. For many women, and especially those whose choice has been taken away as in the case of the survivor of abuse, assertion is a difficult skill to learn. Girls are still not always socialised to expect their 'yes' or 'no' to be heard and respected. I find that this exercise works best when the whole group stands in a circle, so that they are actively reinforcing each other.

Again, a solid upright posture is called for, with a wide base of support. Together, the women are invited to take a good breath in and to say the word 'Yes!' out loud. The therapist can encourage by practising this several times, suggesting each time that the voice becomes stronger, more supported by the diaphragm and not strangled in the throat. It helps to think of an unhindered column of air, rising up from the belly and out into the circle. It is often worth asking whether anyone imagined saying 'yes' to a particular person, or about a particular thing. You can then suggest that everyone think of a time when they wanted their 'yes' to be heard – maybe in an argument, or as a powerful affirmation 'Yes, I do have a right to be heard'. Repeat the exercise once more, with this in mind.

The next stage is to repeat the whole exercise, but this time with 'No!' Finally, discuss as a group which felt easier or more powerful, and why.

Reaching, taking, holding and letting go

The experience of feeling in control of the process of taking, holding and letting go is uncommon for the survivor of abuse. Many have developed ambivalence in relationships, and endings are often particularly difficult. I am indebted to Shirley Summers, Gestalt psychotherapist, for bringing this sequence of movement metaphors to my attention.

The sequence starts with an exploration of arm extension, then reaching. The therapist asks the group to consider, 'What are you reaching towards?' 'Is it a nice feeling, to be reaching towards this, or an uncomfortable or ambivalent (not quite sure) feeling?' 'If uncomfortable or ambivalent, what is that about?' 'Is there something else you would rather reach for?' 'If so, can you do that now, and leave the other thing behind?'

The mover is then invited to take whatever they are reaching towards, if they so choose, and to notice how they do so. Is it with lack of interest? Hurried? Slow and luxuriating? Furtive? What is the quality of that taking?

And so to the holding. Now the mover has what she has reached for, what does she want to do with it? How does she hold it, and where in relation to her body? How does it feel to be doing this?

And finally, the survivor is invited to let go of the object. How is this done? Again, is it hurried or slow? Painful, or a relief? Does she throw it, shake it off, drop it, place it down carefully? How does she feel as she does this?

Following a period of improvisation, it may be useful for each woman to crystallise the exploration into a movement vignette, possibly adding vocalisation.

Finally, I would suggest that the women get together in pairs to discuss their experience, before feeding back to the larger group about the exercise.

Finding a new pathway

This exercise is designed to encourage the group members to evaluate their experience, and begin to look forwards to a time when they will not need the group any longer. I suggest that each woman finds a space in the room, which represents where they feel they are right now on their journey towards recovery. Perhaps they can imagine what the environment in which they have placed themselves might look like, and what they are wearing or carrying with them. Once having established this, I suggest that they take a look backwards, and see where they have come from. In looking back, they are able to see themselves as they were before the group began. What are some of the differences between then and now?

And now, each woman is asked to consider stepping forward on the remainder of her journey, leaving behind the group. What will that journey look like? Is the path straight or winding? What or who might she meet along the way? What might she carry, if anything? What will she take from the group on this journey, and what will she leave behind? How will she move? If she feels ready to do so, the individual is then invited to move physically some of this journey, in order to feel what the future for her will feel like, how she will sit, stand, walk or otherwise move.

Guided imagery: the journey

I find it extremely helpful to write a story for the group, to be read out in the final or penultimate session. The story is a symbolic account of the 'journey' made by the group members during their progress in the group arts therapies programme. This is read aloud to the group members as they relax either on chairs or on the floor, perhaps supported by floor cushions. The tale functions as guided imagery. That is to say, it contains a section at the end, inviting each woman to complete the story for herself in the form of mental pictures. These pictures or images can then be grounded in a drawing or painting, which can be shared with the other group members. Here is an example of such a story:

> It was early springtime when the eight women set out on their journey, a journey that was to take them right through to the end of the summer. They had with them two other women to act as guides. As they met for the start of their journey, the birds sang sweetly and the buds were just forming on the trees.

Each of the eight women had been robbed of something precious, and it was this shared experience which bound them together and made their journey necessary. Each woman needed to reclaim her own land.

The women started by getting to know each other, making agreements that would make their journey as safe as possible. Each woman then stated her vision of where her journey would take her. There were no maps; the women were pioneers, explorers of new uncharted territory. They felt scared, but determined. They discussed what provisions they would need. They agreed to have a good breakfast, and to wrap up warm as the air could still be quite chilly.

On the second leg of their journey, they found a pool. Each woman chose her attire, and her position in or around the pool very carefully. Some of the women bathed in its clear blue waters, to refresh themselves before continuing on their journey.

As they continued, some women began to see that they had been wearing masks. They slowly peeled them off, revealing their true selves to each other.

Together, they wrote a bill of rights that reminded them of the purpose of their journey. They began to take up stances that showed the world 'I am here'. To help them chart their way they made images of where they had been, where they were now, and where they hoped to go.

Gradually, the eight women began to develop a sense of support within their group. From time to time, one or two of the women would need to rest when the going got tough. But as they journeyed, they slowly, one by one, shared their stories; stories that were hard and painful to tell, but which brought a sense of relief and collective strength in the telling.

So they journeyed on, sometimes all together, sometimes without one or another member of their group, who was unable to journey for a short while. Sometimes, one of the guides would be unavailable.

And they began to dance together, at first with uncertain steps, and then delighting in their collective strength as they created a Protection Warrior Dance. They discovered the peace of Menoussis, a Greek circle dance.

Each woman had difficulties in her life while on this journey, and some were ill. They found that the weather expressed and reflected how they felt.

At one point on the journey, the group held a memorial service for one woman's dead grandmother. This grandmother had been her protector, and yet the little girl had been prevented from saying goodbye to her. The whole group helped to lay the grandmother to rest, and to witness the little girl's grief.

From time to time, one or more of the women would feel threatened by a particular man who appeared on the horizon, but the whole group would repel him with their collective strength, using their voices and their gestures to assert their power.

The women told each other of their need to be rescued, of their anger, and of their pain. But sometimes it was hard to trust each other fully, and some of the women felt betrayed. This caused a rift, resulting in the early departure of one of the women.

The betrayal of trust which the woman experienced reminded them of the time when each of them had been robbed. It was necessary for them to talk and draw from their own experience of the child who had been robbed and betrayed, and to examine whether their past and present situations were all good or all bad or a bit of both. They began to re-evaluate who was responsible for what in their lives. Gradually, the trust deepened among the seven women who remained.

Towards the end of the journey, some of the women were collectively able to bring justice upon the men who had robbed them. It was painful to relive their experiences in the trial, but justice brought a new sense of freedom from victimisation.

Finally, they arrived at a place where they could see their journey's end. Before they parted company, they built a camp fire, and each woman took from her back the haversack in which she had been carrying her load throughout the journey. They danced around the fire, a dance of celebration and farewell...

And now, see yourself by the camp fire, having taken off your load and danced together. Open up the haversack, and begin to sift through it. What is in there? What do you still need to carry with you? And what can you dispose of into the fire?...

Watch the flames, burning everything you no longer need. And, as they die down, something new and positive begins to emerge out of the ashes. Watch as this happens...

When you are ready, come back into this room, this body, this time, and slowly open your eyes.

Now, make an image of what you saw emerging from the ashes ...

When you have finished, find a partner to share your image and experience with, before coming back into the circle to share with the others.

Gifts to the self/each other

There are several ways to do this. For example, group members may want to make an art image of a gift that they wish to give to themselves for their future lives. This could be preceded by a guided visualisation, in which the survivor visits a special place where her internal 'wise woman' is waiting to present her with a gift for her future journey. Alternatively, the group could pass around a box, wrapped in gift paper. As each woman receives the box, she could say what she imagines is inside, for her. A third suggestion is that cards could be prepared. Angel cards, obtainable from the Findhorn Foundation (see Appendix 3), are an option, or the therapists and group members can prepare their own together. The cards each will have a quality written on them, for example 'love', 'friendship' or 'assertion', with an accompanying art image perhaps. They are then placed face down on the floor, and each woman chooses one to keep, sharing with the other group members what is written on her card and what this means to her.

Celebration charters

Several A3 sized pieces of paper are laid out on the floor, one with each group member's name at the top. A range of felt-tips is provided, and group members and therapists are encouraged to circulate around the room, writing positive statements about the group member concerned. It is important that these statements are not signed, to avoid the recipient at a later date reading this as 'just so-and-so's opinion'.

Ball of wool

This is one I like to use in the very last session, at the end of the session. I choose a brightly coloured ball of wool, and pass it to a group member, holding on to the end. As I pass her the ball, I tell her something positive I remember about our contact in the group. She then passes the ball to a second person, holding on to her part of the wool as she does so, and herself relates a positive memory about their contact. The process continues, until everyone has finished saying what they need to say to others, forming tangible reminders of the web of connections that exist. After contemplating the image thus created for a while, the procedure is reversed, this time in silence, so that the ball of wool is gradually wound up again, a metaphor for winding up the group.

Evaluation

It is important to evaluate one's work in an ongoing sense, so that services can be continually improved. As a minimum, some of the creative techniques described in this chapter can be used to elicit information on what has or has not been useful to group members. I strongly suggest that in addition where possible, a follow-up session is arranged individually for each group member. This should ideally take place between six and twelve weeks after the last group therapy session. The purpose of the follow-up appointment is to review the individual's progress, discuss strategies for continuing to build on therapeutic change, and assess the usefulness of the intervention. The review form in Figure 7.1 offers a structured way of achieving this. I am grateful to Sue Fletcher (art therapist) for her contribution to the development of the review form.

Summary

In this chapter, I have taken you through the closure and evaluation of your group. You have now completed your first GAT-P for women who have survived the trauma of CSA. It is hoped that a few of those women will feel that they have moved a little further along their journey towards resolution and healing of that trauma. And that you too have survived. In surviving as a therapist, if you have done your job well, you will feel humbled and honoured to have witnessed and stood by the women in your group.

Figure 7.1 – Review form

Name: ....……....................... Date: ....

Introduction: This form is in three parts. The first part will help you to reflect on what the group has meant for you. The second part is about your views on how the group worked together. The third part is for any other comments you may have about the group.

Part One

1. What were your hopes and expectations of the group?

2. Were these hopes and expectations met? If so, how? If not, why do you think this was?

3. Please circle the statement which most closely describes what you do now with the feeling or behaviour listed in the left hand column. (For example, if you feel in control of your anger and able to express it at the right time and place, then put a circle round 'able to express without losing control') As before, if you need to circle more than one statement, please feel free to do so.

Feeling/behaviour			
Anger	keep it in or take it out on myself in some way	able to express without losing control	take it out on others
Sadness	unable to cry or only cry alone	able to cry with someone I trust	out of control or very weepy
Enthusiasm	no enthusiasm	able to feel some enthusiasm	over the top or 'high'
Food	avoiding	eating well	over-eating
Memories of the abuse	buried	aware but not dominating my life	overwhelming or dominating life
Blame for the abuse	blame myself	blame the abuser	blame others
Sense of self-worth	I'm not an OK person	I'm an OK person	I'm a better person than others
Self-assertion	putting my needs last	putting my needs equal to others	putting my needs before others
Relationships	avoiding	balanced/co-operative	dependent

Please rate your own ability to self-assess: Poor • Fair • Good • Very Good
Please note any specific feeling/behaviour which you had difficulty in assessing:

....

4. Since being in the group what do you feel has changed most in the ways you think, feel, behave or relate?

5. What help do you feel you need now?

Part Two

6. Some of the ways we worked together are listed below. Please tick one column for each. If you don't remember doing something, don't tick it at all.

	Very helpful	Helpful	Partly helpful	Not helpful
The 'check-in'				
Making group rules and agreements				
Bill of rights				
Creating a safe place				
Swimming pool				
Using art materials				
Menoussis (Greek circle dance)				
Protection Warrior Dance				
Expressive movement				
Moving between the two parts of the room for different parts of the session				
Using symbolic objects				
Telling your own story				
Hearing others' stories				
Use of photographs				
Charge sheets/trial				
Discussing creative work in the group				
Guided imagery: the journey				
Anything else?				

7. In this group what did you personally find most helpful?

    Can you say why?

8. In this group what did you find least helpful?

    Can you say why?

9. What were the most important challenges you personally faced in the group?

10. What do you think you gained from those challenges?

11. What challenges did you choose not to face?

12. In the ways in which the group therapists worked with the group what did you find:

    (a) most helpful?

    (b) least helpful?

13. From your own experience what would you advise us to do differently next time?

Part Three

14. Please make any other comments about the value of this group to you and/or how the group has been run and worked together.

Finally ... Thank you for completing this form. We hope that you have found it useful in reflecting on how your experience of the group was helpful to you or not.

Please bring the completed form with you to your individual review meeting with the group therapists.

The Research

Introduction

This book arose from my doctoral research at the University of Manchester in north-west England (Meekums 1998). The inquiry was concerned with recovery from the trauma of serious CSA within a GAT-P for women, in a mental health context (Tameside and Glossop Community and Priority Services NHS Trust in north-west England). Seriousness of CSA is often defined by chronicity, intrafamilial perpetrators, physical contact and oral or vaginal penetration (see Chapter 1). For the women who participated in my study, many of these were true. It was also true to say, and more of interest to me as both clinician and researcher, that the women all were suffering mental health symptoms which they found to be disabling, and to which they directly attributed their history of CSA.

The research design

The research design followed one which has been conceptualised as a 'spirallic process of forming' (Meekums 1993). There were four cycles of research, each building on the findings of the previous cycle. Design decisions were ongoing throughout the research, in response to the emerging data and to opportunistic factors, including my own pregnancy which necessitated changes of personnel. Each cycle of the research related to a separate twenty-session GAT-P. Table A1.1 shows the design of each cycle. I took the roles both of researcher and of one of the group therapists during each of the first three cycles. During the fourth cycle, I was unable to facilitate a group due to maternity leave, which provided an opportunity to compare the information received so far with that from a group with whom my relationship was qualitatively different.

Table A1.1 – Research design

	Cycle 1	Cycle 2	Cycle 3	Cycle 4
Number interviewed	3	2	6	3
Modalities	Dramatherapy/ DMT	Dramatherapy/ DMT	Art therapy/ DMT	Art therapy
Researcher as therapist	Yes	Yes	Yes	No

Methodology

The methodology for this inquiry was qualitative, reflexive, broadly participative (Reason 1994) and made use of a modified grounded theory approach (Glaser and Strauss 1967; Strauss and Corbin 1990, 1994). Ethical concerns were a high priority, which meant in practice that:

- Participants were invited to give process consent. This resulted in the sacrifice of some data, when a research participant was not well enough to give her process consent at the stage of return of interview transcripts.
- Levels of participation were flexible, to take account of the vulnerability of participants.
- Those who left the programme were not pursued, which resulted in a sampling bias.
- Identifying characteristics were as far as possible erased in the text.

Procedure

The procedure within each research cycle is shown in Figure A1.1. All interviews were audiotaped and transcribed, then analysed using a coding system adapted from Miles and Huberman (1994).

Summary

This appendix has given a brief overview of the research methodology. More information can be obtained concerning this by consulting either Meekums (1998) or Meekums (1999).

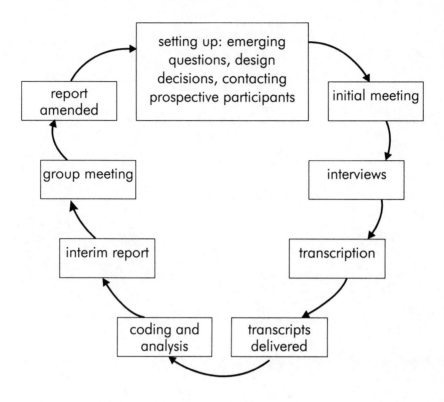

Figure A1.1 – The research cycle

Reliability of assessment in relation to outcome

Introduction

The assessment materials shown in Chapter 4 have been tested over two therapy groups used for the research (cycles 3 and 4), to estimate their usefulness.

Prognosis

The prognoses for these two groups of women using the checklist (Figure 4.6) are shown in Table A2.1. Here, 'group 1' refers to the group of women who volunteered for cycle 3 of the research, and 'group 2' refers to cycle 4.

Table A2.1 – Prognoses at assessment: numbers in each group receiving hopeful, less hopeful or hopeless prognosis

Prognosis	Hopeful	Less hopeful	Hopeless	Total
Group 1	2	4	0	6
Group 2	0	3 (2 of these rated between hopeful and less hopeful)	0	3
Total	2	7	0	9

Measuring outcome

One interesting but qualitative and subjective way to look at outcomes is via the use of the 'landscape' metaphor, described in Chapter 4. The changes observed in six women in their use of the landscape metaphor are shown in Table A2.2. All six of these women had participated in group 1.

Table A2.2 – Changes in landscape (group 1)

Research participant	Initial landscape	Final landscape
Irene	Alone in a desert, no hope.	In a jungle, surrounded by wild animals who could turn at any moment. Temporarily safe by being invisible.
Janine	Not available.	On Kinder Scout (in the Pennine Hills), alone and free, at the top. Raining, could smell the peat.
Jennifer	On a cliff, grey light, feeling confused.	Father on the cliff, she walking through a wood towards a town, where welcomed as a 'long lost member of the human race'.
Madeleine	On a hill, wanting to embark on a journey, holding her teddy.	With teddy, in the centre of a tornado, spinning and spiralling upwards (2–3 weeks earlier, would have been Julie Andrews on a hill top).
Terry	On the edge of a rubbish dump, wanting mother to help her away from the edge, but no help. Tried the other side and retreated to the familiar.	In a wheatfield, entering by unfenced area and walking past the middle towards the fence. Peaceful, smelt the wheat, unafraid.
Yvonne	On a beach, happy, suddenly needing to shed tears. Relief, ending with watching the sea.	On a beach, alone, running about and happy. Blue sky and water, could do any thing she wanted. Beautiful.

Outcomes in relation to initial prognosis are shown in Tables A2.3 (group 1) and A2.4 (group 2). These outcomes were assessed using interview data, the review form (Figure 7.1) and, in the case of the first of the two groups, clinical data since I was also one of the group therapists for this group.

Table A2.3 – Outcomes for group 1

Identification	Prognosis	Outcome	Comments
Irene	2	2	cutting off from feelings and from support
Janine	2	2	long history of very severe abuse, said she needed more disclosure
Jennifer	1	1	acceptance of memory gaps, addressed important issues
Madeleine	1	1	asking for more therapy for the next stage
Terry	2	2	exceeded expectations (had been suicidal but stopped self-harming), high level of support
Yvonne	2	1	previous and ongoing help +++, significant grieving in group

Key

Names are pseudonyms.

Numbers refer to the rating given:

1 = hopeful prognosis. Outcome indicating a reduction in symptoms likely to lead to a reduction in involvement of the mental health services.

2 = less hopeful prognosis. Outcome indicating either a reduction in symptoms which is unlikely to be maintained without continued or increased levels of support from the mental health services, no reduction in symptoms or a worsening of symptoms.

Table A2.4 – Outcomes for group 2

Identification	Prognosis	Outcome	Comments
Joan	1/2	2	crisis after programme, undeveloped relationship with key worker
Rose	1/2	1/2	small but permanent gains, very severe abuse but individual therapy +++
Alice	2	2	small but significant and fundamental change

Key

Names are pseudonyms.

Numbers refer to the rating given:

1 = hopeful prognosis. Outcome indicating a reduction in symptoms likely to lead to a reduction in involvement of the mental health services.

2 = less hopeful prognosis. Outcome indicating either a reduction in symptoms which is unlikely to be maintained without continued or increased levels of support from the mental health services, no reduction in symptoms or a worsening of symptoms.

The accuracy of predictions made using the checklist (Figure 4.7) was roughly equal across the two groups despite group 2 containing clients whose prognoses were less favourable than those for group 1. Table A2.3 shows that the therapists predicted incorrectly in one case for group 1, giving a less favourable prognosis than the outcome. In this case, the client had received a high level of support from her key worker during the GAT-P. Table A2.4 shows that the therapists also predicted incorrectly in one case for group 2. This time they had rated her as between 1 and 2, but the outcome was a definite 2, with a worsening of her symptoms. This woman told the researcher that she had not had a fully developed therapeutic alliance with her key worker prior to the start of the programme, although this had since developed. Although one must be cautious in interpreting data from two cases, the relationship with the key worker was found to be important in the wider research study in providing the required sense of safety prior to addressing painful issues in group therapy. As discussed in Chapter 3, if the necessary sense of safety (derived from a complex interaction of key worker involvement, therapist style, group factors and life situation) is not available to the survivor she can make little use of the GAT-P. At worst, she may even experience an increase in her symptoms.

The nature of outcomes in these same two groups is summarised in Table A2.5. The following overall trends in outcomes can be observed from an examination of this data is:

- a reduction in self-harming

- an increased sense of the future

- an increased sense of self-worth

- an increased ability to behave assertively

- an increased tendency to place the blame with the abuser

- a reduction in intrusive imagery

- minimal changes in relation to sex and feelings, and no change in relation to food. Such trends as are observable may indicate an increase in feeling, including sexual feeling.

Table A2.5 – Nature of outcomes aggregated over groups 1 and 2

Variable	Before		After	
1 Risk				
Self-harming	Yes:	5	Yes:	3
	No:	4	No:	6
Sense of future	Yes:	2	Yes:	5
	No:	7	No:	4
2 Ego strength				
Self-worth	I'm OK:	2	I'm OK:	6
	I'm not OK:	7	I'm not OK:	3
Self-assertion	Assertive:	0	Assertive:	6
	Passive:	7	Passive:	2
	Aggressive:	2	Aggressive:	1
Blame for abuse	Abuser:	3	Abuser:	7
	Self:	6	Self:	2
3 Embodiment				
Sex	Avoid:	4	Avoid:	4
	Difficult:	4	Difficult:	3
	OK:	1	OK:	2
Food	OK:	5	OK:	5
	Problematic:	4	Problematic:	4
Feelings (emotions)	OK:	1	OK:	4
	Buried:	2	Buried:	0
	Overwhelming	6	Overwhelming	5
4 Intrusive imagery	Yes:	6	Yes:	3
	No:	3	No:	6

Key

Numbers shown are the number of women out of a total of nine.

Discussion

The outcomes cannot be seen to be statistically significant, since the sample size was small; there was no control group; and non-standardised ways of eliciting the information were used including qualitative data from interviews. Neither can a causal relationship be assumed. However, while not proven as valid and reliable research tools, it may be tentatively concluded that the assessment materials used, and the checklist derived from these, have some clinical value in predicting outcome provided that other tried and tested assessment methods are also followed. Following this kind of therapeutic programme, some benefits can be expected for some women in terms of reduced risk to self, increased ego strength and reduction in intrusive imagery. Changes on a bodily level, however, including changes in sexual dysfunction, eating disorders and dissociative disorders, appear to be more resistant to this kind of intervention. It is not clear whether a longer term intervention or individual arts therapies would produce any further change, or whether a different modality, for example cognitive behavioural therapy, might better address these issues as part of an ongoing package of care.

Useful contacts

Arts therapies organisations

Association for Dance Movement Therapy (UK)
c/o Quaker Meeting House
Wedmore Vale
Bristol BS3 5HX
email: query@dmtuk.co.uk
website: http://www.dmtuk.demon.co.uk

Association of Professional Music Therapists
Diana Asbridge, Administrator
26 Hamlyn Road
Glastonbury
Somerset
BA6 8HT

British Association of Art Therapists
Mary Ward House
5 Tavistock Place
London WC1H 9SN
Tel: 020 7383 3774
Fax: 020 7387 5513

British Association of Dramatherapists
Registered Office
41 Broomhouse Lane
Hurlingham Park
London SW6 3DP

Organisations providing help to survivors of CSA

Careline	020 8514 1177
Childline	0800 1111
NSPCC	0800 800 500
NSPCC Minicom	0800 056 0566
Refuge 24-hour National Crisis Line	0990 995 443
The Samaritans (lo-call)	0345 90 90 90
Shelterline	0808 800 4444
Victim Support (lo-call)	0845 30 30 900
Welsh Women's Aid	01222 390 874
Women's Aid National Domestic Violence Helpline (lo-call)	0345 023 468

Other organisations

British Psychodrama and Sociodrama Association
Jane Scanlon, Administrator
Heather Cottage
The Clachan
Roseneath
Hellensburgh
Argyle
Bute
Scotland G84 ORF

Findhorn Foundation
The Park
Forres
Scotland IV36 OTZ

This space is provided for you to write down local contact numbers
Tip: include Rape Crisis, NHS and Social Services numbers, Relate, and specialist services.

This space is provided for you to write down your local contact numbers.

Further reading

Arts therapies

Chodorow, J. (1991) *Dance Therapy and Depth Psychology.* London: Routledge.

Jennings, S. (ed) (1975) *Creative Therapy.* London: Pitman.

Jennings, S. (ed) (1987) *Dramatherapy, Theory and Practice for Teachers and Clinicians.* London: Routledge.

Jennings, S. (1990) *Dramatherapy with Families, Groups and Individuals.* London: Jessica Kingsley Publishers.

Jennings, S. and Minde, A. (1993) *Art Therapy and Dramatherapy: Masks of the Soul.* London: Jessica Kingsley Publishers.

Payne, H. (ed) (1992) *Dance Movement Therapy: Theory and Practice.* London: Tavistock/Routledge.

Payne, H. (ed) (1993) *Handbook of Inquiry in the Arts Therapies: One River, Many Currents.* London: Jessica Kingsley Publishers.

Stanton-Jones, K. (1992) *Dance Movement Therapy in Psychiatry.* London: Tavistock/Routledge.

Waller, D. and Gilroy, A. (eds) (1992) *Art Therapy: A Handbook.* Buckingham: Open University Press.

Warren, B. (ed) (1984) *Using the Creative Arts in Therapy.* London: Routledge.

Wethered, A.G. (1973) *Drama and Movement in Therapy.* London: MacDonald & Evans.

Child sexual abuse and self-perservation

Bannister, A. (ed) (1998) *From Hearing to Healing: Working with the Aftermath of Child Sexual Abuse,* 2nd edn. London: Longman.

Quinn, K. (1983) *Stand Your Ground: A Woman's Guide to Self-Preservation.* London: Orbis.

References

Agger, I. and Jensen, S.B. (1990) 'Testimony as ritual evidence in psychotherapy for political refugees.' *Journal of Traumatic Stress 3*, 115–130. Cited in J.L. Herman (1992) *Trauma and Recovery*. New York: Basic Books.

Aldridge, D., Brandt, G. and Wohler, D. (1990) 'Toward a common language among the creative art therapies.' *The Arts in Psychotherapy 17*, 3, 189–195.

Alexander, P.C. (1992) 'Application of attachment theory to the study of sexual abuse.' *Journal of Consulting and Clinical Psychology 60*, 2, 185–195.

Alexander, P.C., Neimeyer, R.A., Follette, V.M., Moore, M.K. and Harter, S. (1989) 'A comparison of group treatments of women sexually abused as children.' *Journal of Consulting and Clinical Psychology 57*, 4, 479–483.

Ambra, L.N. (1995) 'Approaches used in dance/movement therapy with adult incest survivors.' *American Journal of Dance Therapy 17*, 1, 15–24.

American Psychiatric Association (1980) *Diagnostic and Statistical Manual of Psychiatric Disorders, Vol 3* (DSM-III). Washington, DC: American Psychiatric Association.

American Psychiatric Association (1994) *Diagnostic Criteria from DSM-IV.* Washington, DC: American Psychiatric Association.

Anderson, F.E. (1995) 'Catharsis and empowerment through group claywork with incest survivors.' *The Arts in Psychotherapy 22*, 5, 413–427.

Angelou, M. (1984) *I Know Why the Caged Bird Sings.* London: Virago.

Angus, L.E. and Rennie, D.L. (1989) 'Envisioning the representational world: the client's experience of metaphoric expression in psychotherapy.' *Psychotherapy 26*, 3, 372–379.

Axline, V.M. (1964) *Dibs in Search of Self: Personality Development in Play Therapy.* Harmondsworth: Penguin.

Bagley, C. (1990) 'Is the prevalence of child sexual abuse decreasing? Evidence from a random sample of 750 young adult women.' *Psychological Reports 66*, 1037–1038.

Bagley, C. (1995) A typology of child sexual abuse: addressing the paradox of interlocking emotional, physical and sexual abuse as causes of adult psychiatric sequels in women. Unpublished paper given to Annual Conference of the Canadian Sex Research Forum, Banff, October.

Bagley, C. and Ramsey, R. (1986) 'Sexual abuse in childhood: psychosocial outcomes and implications for social work practice.' *Journal of Social Work and Human Sexuality 4*, 1–2, 33–47.

Bagley, C.R. and Young, L. (1990) 'Depression, self-esteem, and suicidal behaviour as sequels of sexual abuse in childhood: research and therapy.' In M. Rothery and G. Cameron (eds) *Child Maltreatment: Expanded Concepts of Helping.* New York: Erlbaum.

Bagley, C., Wood, M. and Young, L. (1994) 'Victim to abuser: mental health and behavioral sequels of child sexual abuse in a community survey of young adult males.' *Child Abuse and Neglect 18*, 8, 683–697.

Baker, A.W. and Duncan, S.P. (1985) 'Child sexual abuse: a study of prevalence in Great Britain.' *Child Abuse and Neglect 9*, 457–467.

Bannister, A. (1991) 'Learning to live again: psychodramatic techniques with sexually abused young people.' In P. Holmes and M. Karp (eds) *Psychodrama: Inspiration and Technique.* London: Tavistock/Routledge.

Bass, E. and Davis, L. (1988) *The Courage to Heal.* London: Harper & Row.

Battle, J. (1981) *Culture-Free SEI Self-Esteem Inventories for Children and Adults.* Seattle, WA: Special Child Publications.

Beck, A. (1978) *Beck Inventory.* Philadelphia, PA: Centre for Cognitive Therapy.

Beitchman, J.H., Zucker, K.J., Hood, J.E., da Costa, G.A., Akman, D. and Cassavia, E. (1992) 'A review of the long-term effects of child sexual abuse.' *Child Abuse and Neglect 16*, 101–118.

Berrol, C. (1992) 'The neurophysiologic basis of the mind-body connection in dance/movement therapy.' *American Journal of Dance Therapy 14*, 1, 19–29.

Berry, M. (1997) 'What practitioners can learn from the research regarding the long term effects of child sexual abuse.' *British Association of Counselling Research Paper no. 2.* Paper given at the Annual General Conference of the British Association of Counselling, Warwick, 8 September 1995.

Billow, R.M. (1977) 'Metaphor: a review of the psychological literature.' *Psychological Bulletin 84*, 1, 81–92.

Birtchnell, J. (1984) 'Art therapy as a form of psychotherapy.' In T. Dalley (ed) *Art as Therapy: An Introduction to the Use of Art as a Therapeutic Technique.* London: Tavistock/Routledge.

Blatner, A. (1991) 'Theoretical principles underlying creative arts therapies.' *The Arts in Psychotherapy 18*, 5, 405–409.

Blatt, J. (1991) 'Dance/movement therapy: inherent value of the creative process in psychotherapy.' In G.D. Wilson (ed) *Psychology and Performing Arts.* Amsterdam: Swets & Zerlinger.

Bloch, S. and Crouch, E. (1987) *Therapeutic Factors in Group Psychotherapy.* Oxford: Oxford University Press.

Blume, E.S. (1990) *Secret Survivors: Uncovering Incest and its After-effects in Women.* Chichester: Wiley.

Boden, M. (1990) *The Creative Mind: Myths and Mechanisms.* London: Weidenfeld and Nicolson.

Brière, J. (1992) 'Methodological issues in the study of sexual abuse effects.' *Journal of Consulting and Clinical Psychology 60,* 2, 196–203.

Brière, J. and Runtz, M. (1988) 'Symptomatology associated with childhood sexual victimization in a nonclinical adult sample.' *Child Abuse and Neglect 12,* 51–59.

Brière, J. and Runtz, M. (1989) 'The trauma symptom checklist (TSC–33): early data on a new scale.' *Journal of Interpersonal Violence 4,* 2, 151–165.

Brooke, S.L. (1995a) 'Art therapy: an approach to working with sexual abuse survivors.' *The Arts in Psychotherapy 22,* 5, 447–466.

Brooke, S.L. (1995b) 'A critical review of Battle's Culture-Free Self-Esteem Inventory.' *Measurement and Evaluation in Counselling and Development 27,* 4, 248–252.

Brooks, D. and Stark, A. (1989) 'The effect of dance/movement therapy on affect: a pilot study.' *American Journal of Dance Therapy 11,* 2, 101–112.

Brown, G.R. and Anderson, B. (1991) 'Psychiatric morbidity in adult inpatients with childhood histories of sexual and physical abuse.' *American Journal of Psychiatry 148,* 1, 55–61.

Browne, A. and Finkelhor, D. (1986) 'Impact of child sexual abuse: a review of the research.' *Psychological Bulletin 99,* 1, 66–77.

Burns, D. and Nolen-Hoeksema, S. (1992) 'Therapeutic empathy and recovery from depression in cognitive-behavioral therapy: a structural equation model.' *Journal of Consulting and Clinical Psychology 60,* 3, 441–449.

Byrd, K.R. (1995) 'The myth of psyche and cupid as an allegory for survivors of child sexual abuse.' *The Arts in Psychotherapy 22,* 5, 403–411.

Cahill, C., Llewelyn, S.P. and Pearson, C. (1991) 'Treatment of sexual abuse which occurred in childhood: a review.' *British Journal of Clinical Psychology 30,* 1–12.

Campling, P. and Culverwell, A. (1990) 'Themes of abuse: neglect and intrusion.' *Changes 8,* 2, 119–128.

Capra, F. (1976) *The Tao of Physics.* London: Fontana.

Case, C. and Dalley, T. (1990) 'Introduction.' In C. Case and T. Dalley (eds) *Working with Children in Art Therapy.* London: Routledge.

Christrup, H.J. (1962) 'The effect of dance therapy on the concept of body image.' *Psychiatric Quarterly Supplement 2,* 36, 296–303.

Chu, J.A. and Dill, D.L. (1990) 'Dissociative symptoms in relation to childhood physical and sexual abuse.' *American Journal of Psychiatry 147*, 7, 887–892.

Cienfuegos, A.J. and Monelli, C. (1983) 'The testimony of political repression as a therapeutic instrument.' *American Journal of Orthopsychiatry 53*, 43–51. Cited in J.L. Herman (1992) *Trauma and Recovery.* New York: Basic Books.

Condon, W.S. and Sander, L.W. (1974) 'Neonate movement is synchronised with adult speech: inter-actional participation and language acquisition.' *Science 183*, 99–101.

Courtois, C. (1988) *Healing the Incest Wound.* New York: Norton.

Cox, M. and Theilgaard, A. (1987) *Mutative Metaphors in Psychotherapy: The Aeolian Mode.* London: Tavistock.

Craine, L.S., Henson, C.E., Colliver, J.A. and MacLean, D.G. (1988) 'Prevalence of a history of sexual abuse among female psychiatric patients in a state hospital system.' *Hospital and Community Psychiatry 39*, 3, 300–304.

Cruz, R.F. and Sabers, D.L. (1998) 'Letter: Dance/movement therapy is more effective than previously reported.' *The Arts in Psychotherapy 25*, 2, 101–104.

Dalley, T. (1997) 'Art therapy. In NSPCC,' *Turning Points: A Resource Pack for Communicating with Children.* London: NSPCC.

Darongkamas, J., Madden, S., Swarbrick, P. and Evans, B. (1995) 'The touchstone therapy group for women survivors of child sexual abuse.' *Journal of Mental Health 4*, 17–29.

Dempster, H.L. and Roberts, J. (1991) 'Child sexual abuse research: a methodological quagmire.' *Child Abuse and Neglect 15*, 593–595.

Den Herder, D. and Redner, L. (1991) 'The treatment of childhood sexual trauma in chronically mentally ill adults.' *Health and Social Work 16*, 1, 50–57.

Dent-Brown, K. (1993) 'Child sexual abuse: problems for adult survivors.' *Journal of Mental Health 2*, 329–338.

Derogatis, L.R. (1983) *The SCL–90–R Manual II: Administration, Scoring and Procedures.* Towson, MD: Clinical Psychometric Research.

Derogatis, L., Lipman, R. and Covi, L. (1973) 'SCL–90: an outpatient psychiatric rating scale – preliminary report.' *Psychopharmacology Bulletin 9*, 13–17.

Dubowski, J. (1990) 'Art versus language (separate development during childhood).' In C. Case and T. Dalley (eds) *Working with Children in Art Therapy.* London: Routledge.

Finkelhor, D. (1979) *Sexually Victimized Children.* New York: Free Press.

Finkelhor, D. (1986) *A Sourcebook on Child Sexual Abuse.* London: Sage.

Finkelhor, D. (1994) 'The international epidemiology of child sexual abuse.' *Child Abuse and Neglect 18*, 5, 409–417.

Finkelhor, D. and Browne, A. (1985) 'The traumatic impact of child sexual abuse: a conceptualization.' *American Journal of Orthopsychiatry 55*, 4, 530–541.

Fisher, P.M., Winnie, P.H. and Ley, R.G. (1993) 'Group therapy for adult survivors of child sexual abuse: differentiation of completers versus dropouts.' *Psychotherapy 30*, 616–623.

Follette, V.M., Alexander, P.C. and Follette, W.C. (1991) 'Individual predictors of outcome in group treatment for incest survivors.' *Journal of Consulting and Clinical Psychology 59*, 1, 150–155.

Fonagy, P. and Target, M. (1995) Memories of abuse: psychological and psychoanalytical perspectives. Unpublished paper presented at 'Memories of Abuse', Universities Psychotherapy Association Annual Conference, Sheffield, 14 December.

Fox, M. (1983) *Original Blessing.* Santa Fe, NM: Bear.

Freud, S. (1896) 'The aetiology of hysteria' (translated by James Strachey), read before the Society for Psychiatry and Neurology, Vienna, 21 April. Reprinted in J. Masson (1992) *The Assault on Truth: Freud and Child Sexual Abuse.* London: Fontana.

Fromuth, M.E. (1986) 'The relationship of childhood sexual abuse with later psychological and sexual adjustment in a sample of college women.' *Child Abuse and Neglect 10*, 5–15.

Fulkerson, M. (1982) 'The move to stillness.' *Dartington Theatre Papers*, 4th series, 10.

Gelinas, D.J. (1983) 'The persisting negative effects of incest.' *Psychiatry 46*, 312–332.

Gendlin, E.T. (1962) *Experiencing and the Creation of Meaning.* New York: Free Press.

Gendlin, E.T. (1981) *Focusing,* 2nd edn. New York: Bantam.

Gerrard, N. (1997) 'Into the arms of the abusers.' *Observer* 25 May, 3–4.

Glaser, B. and Strauss, A.L. (1967) *The Discovery of Grounded Theory: Strategies for Qualitative Research.* Chicago: Aldine.

Gordon, R. (1975) 'The creative process: self-expression and self-transcendence.' In S. Jennings (ed) *Creative Therapy.* London: Pitman.

Gorelick, K. (1989) 'Rapprochement between the arts and psychotherapies: metaphor the mediator.' *The Arts in Psychotherapy 16*, 149–155.

Grainger, R. (1990) *Drama and Healing: The Roots of Drama Therapy.* London: Jessica Kingsley Publishers.

Grant, L. (1994) 'Listen up, dad, these memories are not false.' *Observer* 15 May, 21.

Green, A.H. (1993) 'Child sexual abuse: immediate and longterm effects and intervention.' *Journal of American Academic Child Adolescent Psychiatry 32*, 5, 890–901.

Greig, E. and Betts, T. (1992) 'Epileptic seizures induced by sexual abuse: pathogenic and pathoplastic factors.' *Seizure 1*, 269–274.

Grenadier, S. (1995) 'The place wherein truth lies: an expressive therapy perspective on trauma, innocence and human nature.' *The Arts in Psychotherapy 22*, 5, 393–402.

Gross, R.J., Doerr, H., Caldirola, D., Guzinski, G.M. and Ripley, H.S. (1980) 'Borderline syndrome and incest in chronic pelvic pain patients.' *International Journal of Psychiatry in Medicine 10*, 1, 79–96.

Hackman, A. (1999) Talk for the British Association for Behavioural and Cognitive Psychotherapies North-West, Withington Hospital, Manchester, 10 May.

Hadamard, J. (1954) *The Psychology of Invention in the Mathematical Field.* London: Dover.

Hagood, M. (1990) 'Reflections: art therapy research in England: impressions of an American art therapist.' *The Arts in Psychotherapy 17*, 1, 75–80.

Hagood, M.M. (1992) 'Status of child sexual abuse in the United Kingdom and implications for British Art Therapists.' *Inscape* spring, 27–33.

Hall, Z., Mullee, M. and Thompson, C. (1995) 'A clinical and service evaluation of group therapy for women survivors of childhood sexual abuse.' In M. Aveline and D. Shapiro (eds) *Research Foundations for Psychotherapy Practice.* Chichester: Wiley.

Hamilton, M. (1967) 'Development of a rating scale for primary depressive illness.' *British Journal of Psychiatry 6*, 278–296.

Hazzard, A., Rogers, J.H. and Angert, L. (1993) 'Factors affecting group therapy outcome for adult sexual abuse survivors.' *International Journal of Group Psychotherapy 45*, 4, 453–468.

Herman, J.L. (1992) *Trauma and Recovery.* New York: Basic Books.

Herman, J., Russell, D. and Trocki, K. (1986) 'Long-term effects of incestuous abuse in childhood.' *American Journal of Psychiatry 143*, 10, 1293–1296.

Hossack, A. and Bentall, R. (1996) 'Elimination of posttraumatic symptomatology by relaxation and visual-kinesthetic dissociation.' *Journal of Traumatic Stress 9*, 1, 99–110.

Hudson, W. (1982) *The Clinical Measurement Package: A Field Manual.* Chicago: Dorsey.

Hulme, P.A. and Grove, S.K. (1994) 'Symptoms of female survivors of child sexual abuse.' *Issues in Mental Health Nursing 15*, 5, 519–532.

Hunt, H. and Bledin, K. (1992) 'A different experience of running a group for sexually abused women: a response to Campling and Culverwell.' *Changes 10*, 1, 15–23.

Jehu, D., Gazan, M. and Klassen, C. (1988) *Beyond Sexual Abuse: Therapy with Women Who Were Childhood Victims.* London: Wiley.

Jennings, S. (1993) 'My journey into dramatherapy.' In S. Jennings and A. Minde (eds) *Art Therapy and Dramatherapy: Masks of the Soul.* Jessica Kingsley Publishers.

Jennings, S. (1996) 'Brief dramatherapy: the healing power of the dramatized here and now.' In A. Gersie (ed) *Dramatic Approaches to Brief Therapy.* London: Jessica Kingsley Publishers.

Johnson, D.R. (1988) 'Introduction to the special issue: creative arts therapists as contemporary shamans – reality or romance?' *The Arts in Psychotherapy 15*, 4, 269–270.

Jones, E. (1991) *Working with Adult Survivors of Childhood Abuse.* London: Karnac.

Jones, P. (1996) *Drama as Therapy, Theatre as Living.* London: Routledge.

Jumper, S.A. (1995) 'A meta-analysis of the relationship of child sexual abuse to adult psychological adjustment.' *Child Abuse and Neglect 19*, 6, 715–728.

Kane, E. (1989) *Recovering from Incest: Imagination and the Healing Process.* Boston, MA: Sigo Press.

Karp, M. (1991) 'Psychodrama and picalilli: residential treatment of a sexually abused adult.' In P. Holmes and M. Karp (eds) *Psychodrama: Inspiration and Technique.* London: Tavistock/Routledge.

Keane, T.M., Fairbank, J.A., Caddell, J.M. *et al.* (1989) 'Implosive (flooding) therapy reduces symptoms of PTSD in Vietnam combat veterans.' *Behaviour Therapy 20*, 245–260. Cited in J.L. Herman (1992) *Trauma and Recovery.* New York: Basic Books.

Kline, F., Burgoyne, R., Staples, F., Moredock, P., Snyder, V. and Joerger, M. (1977) 'A report on the use of movement therapy for chronic, severely disabled outpatients.' *Art Psychotherapy 4*, 181–183.

Koestler, A. (1964) *The Act of Creation.* London: Picador.

Kuettel, T. (1982) 'Affective change in dance therapy.' *American Journal of Dance Therapy 5*, 56–64.

Lakoff, G. and Johnson, M. (1980) *Metaphors We Live By.* London: University of Chicago Press.

Lambert, M.J., Bergin, A.E. and Collins, J.L. (1977) 'Therapist-induced deterioration in psychotherapy.' In A.S. Gurman and A.M. Razin (eds) *Effective Psychotherapy: A Handbook of Research.* Oxford: Pergamon.

Landy, R.J. (1996) *Essays in Drama Therapy.* London: Jessica Kingsley Publishers.

Lansley, J. (1977) 'Off our toes.' *Spare Rib 64*, November, 5–8.

Lesté, A. and Rust, J. (1984) 'Effects of dance on anxiety.' *Perceptual and Motor Skills 58*, 767–772.

Levens, M. (1994) 'The use of guided fantasy in art therapy with survivors of sexual abuse.' *The Arts in Psychotherapy 21*, 2, 127–134.

Levy, F. (1992) *Dance Movement Therapy: A Healing Art*, revised edn. Reston, VA: American Alliance for Health, Physical Education, Recreation and Dance.

Lewis, P.P. (1988) 'Clinical focus: the transformative process within the imaginal realm.' *The Arts in Psychotherapy 15*, 4, 309–316.

Loftus, E.F. (1994) 'The repressed memory controversy.' *American Psychologist 49*, May, 443–445.

Low, K.G. and Ritter, M. (1998) 'Letter: response to Cruz and Sabers.' *The Arts in Psychotherapy 25*, 2, 105–107.

Luborsky, L., Crits-Christoph, P., Mintz, J. and Auerbach, A. (1988) *Who Will Benefit from Psychotherapy? Predicting Therapeutic Outcomes.* New York: Basic Books.

McClelland, L., Mynors-Wallis, L., Fahy, T. and Treasure, J. (1991) 'Sexual abuse, disordered personality and eating disorders.' *British Journal of Psychiatry 158* (suppl.10), 63–68.

Mackay, B., Gold, M. and Gold, E.A. (1987) 'A pilot study in drama therapy with adolescent girls who have been sexually abused.' *The Arts in Psychotherapy 14*, 1, 77–84.

McLeod, J. (1990) 'The client's experience of counselling and psychotherapy: a review of the research literature.' In D. Mearns and W. Dryden (eds) *Experience of Counselling in Action.* London: Sage.

McLeod, J. (1996) 'The emerging narrative approach to counselling and psychotherapy.' *British Journal of Guidance and Counselling 24*, 2, 173–184.

MacLeod, A.K., Williams, J.M.G. and Linehan, M.M. (1992) 'New developments in the understanding and treatment of suicidal behaviour.' *Behavioural Psychotherapy 20*, 193–218.

McMillen, C., Zuravin, S. and Rideout, G. (1995) 'Perceived benefit from child sexual abuse.' *Journal of Consulting and Clinical Psychology 63*, 6, 1037–1043.

Mahler, M. (1979) *The Selected Papers of Margaret Mahler, Volume 2, Separation-Individuation.* New York: Jason Aronson.

Maltz, W. and Holman, B. (1987) *Incest and Sexuality: A Guide to Understanding and Healing.* Lexington, MA: Heath.

Masson, J. (1992) *The Assault on Truth: Freud and Child Sexual Abuse.* London: Fontana.

May, P., Wesler, M., Salkin, J. and Schoop, T. (1974) 'Non-verbal techniques in the re-establishment of body image and self-identity – a report.' In M.N. Costonis (ed) *Therapy in Motion.* Chicago: University of Illinois Press.

May, R. (1975) *The Courage to Create.* London: Collins.

Meekums, B. (1988) 'Dance movement therapy and the development of mother–child interaction: a pilot study.' *Proceedings of Dance and the Child International Conference.* London: Roehampton Institute.

Meekums, B. (1990) Dance movement therapy and the development of mother–child interaction. Unpublished MPhil thesis, University of Manchester.

Meekums, B. (1991) 'Dance movement therapy with mothers and young children at risk of abuse.' *The Arts in Psychotherapy 18*, 3, 223–230.

Meekums, B. (1992) 'The Love Bugs: dance movement therapy in a Family Service Unit.' In H. Payne (ed) *Dance Movement Therapy: Theory and Practice.* London: Routledge.

Meekums, B. (1993) 'Research as an act of creation.' In H. Payne (ed) *Handbook of Inquiry in the Arts Therapies: One River, Many Currents.* London: Jessica Kingsley Publishers.

Meekums, B. (1995) 'The dilemma of embodiment for survivors of child sexual abuse.' *Association for Dance Movement Therapy Newsletter 7*, 4, 8–10.

Meekums, B. (1996) Unpublished caseload audit for Tameside and Glossop Community and Priority Trust, Psychotherapy Service.

Meekums, B. (1998) Recovery from child sexual abuse trauma within an arts therapies programme for women. Unpublished PhD thesis, University of Manchester Faculty of Education.

Meekums, B. (1999) 'A creative model for recovery from child sexual abuse trauma.' *The Arts in Psychotherapy 26*, 4.

Miles, M.B. and Huberman, A.M. (1994) *An Expanded Sourcebook of Qualitative Data Analysis*, 2nd edn. London: Sage.

Miller, J., Moeller, D., Kaufman, A., Divasto, P., Pathak, D. and Christy, J. (1978) 'Recidivism among sex assault victims.' *American Journal of Psychiatry 139*, 9, 1103–1104.

Millon, T. (1983) *Millon Clinical Multiaxial Inventory Manual*, 3rd edn. Minneapolis, MN: Interpretive Scoring System.

Milner, M. (1952) 'Aspects of symbolism in the comprehension of the not-self.' *International Journal of Psychoanalysis 33*, 181–195.

Minde, A. (1993) 'My journey into art therapy.' In S. Jennings and A. Minde, *Art Therapy and Dramatherapy: Masks of the Soul.* London: Jessica Kingsley Publishers.

Mitchell, K.M., Bozarth, J.D. and Krauft, C.C. (1977) 'A reappraisal of the therapeutic effectiveness of accurate empathy, nonpossessive warmth, and genuineness.' In A.S. Gurman and A.M. Razin (eds) *Effective Psychotherapy: A Handbook of Research.* Oxford: Pergamon.

Morrison, J. (1989) 'Childhood sexual histories of women with somatization disorder.' *American Journal of Psychiatry 142*, 2, 239–241.

Morton, J. (1994) 'Let's not make up our minds.' *Guardian* 14 May, 26.

Morton, J., Andrews, B., Bekerian, D., Brewin, C., Davies, G. and Mollon, P. (1995) *Recovered Memories: Report of the Working Party of the British Psychological Society.* Leicester: British Psychological Society.

Mrazek, P.J., Lynch, M.A. and Bentovim, A. (1983) 'Sexual abuse of children in the United Kingdom.' *Child Abuse and Neglect 7,* 147–153.

Mullen, P.E., Martin, J.L., Anderson, J.C., Romans, S.E. and Herbison, G.P. (1994) 'The effect of child sexual abuse on social, interpersonal and sexual function in adult life.' *British Journal of Psychiatry 165,* 35–47.

Nash, C.L. and West, D.J. (1985) 'Sexual molestation of young girls: a retrospective survey.' In D.J. West (ed) *Sexual Victimisation.* Aldershot: Gower.

Neimeyer, R.A. (1988) 'Clinical guidelines for conducting interpersonal transaction groups.' *International Journal for Personal Construct Psychology 1,* 181–190.

Nez, D. (1991) 'Persephone's return: archetypal art therapy and the treatment of a survivor of abuse.' *The Arts in Psychotherapy 18,* 2, 123–130.

Nowicki, S. and Duke, M.P. (1974) 'A locus of control scale for college as well as non-college adults.' *Journal of Personality Assessment 38,* 136–137.

Olafson, E., Corwin, D.L. and Summit, R.C. (1993) 'Modern history of child sexual abuse awareness: cycles of discovery and suppression.' *Child Abuse and Neglect 17,* 7–24.

Olesen, V. (1994) 'Feminisms and models of qualitative research.' In N.K. Denzin and Y.S. Lincoln (eds) *Handbook of Qualitative Research.* London: Sage.

Palmer, R.L., Coleman, L., Chaloner, D., Oppenheimer, R. and Smith, J. (1993) 'Childhood sexual experiences with adults: a comparison of reports by women psychiatric patients and general practice attenders.' *British Journal of Psychiatry 163,* 499–504.

Parks, P. (1990) *Rescuing the Inner Child.* London: Souvenir Press.

Parry, G. and Richardson, A. (1996) *NHS Psychotherapy Services in England: Review of Strategic Policy.* NHS Executive, Wetherby: Department of Health.

Pendzik, S. (1988) 'Dramatherapy on abuse: a descent to the underworld.' *Journal of British Association for Dramatherapists 1,* 2, 21–28.

Perris, C., Jacobson, L., Linstrom, H., Van Knorring, L. and Perris, H. (1980) 'Development of a new inventory for assessing memories of parental rearing behaviour.' *Acta Psychiatrica Scandinavica 61,* 265–274.

Peterson, B. and Cameron, C. (1978) 'Preparing high anxiety patients for psychotherapy through body therapy.' *Journal of Contemporary Psychotherapy 9,* 2, 171–177.

Poincaré, H. (1982) 'Mathematical creation.' In H. Poincaré, *The Foundations of Science: Science and Hypothesis, the Value of Science, Science and Method.* Washington, DC: University Press of America.

Puretz, S.L. (1978) 'A comparison of the effects of dance and physical education on the self-concept of selected disadvantaged girls.' *Dance Research Annual 11, Psychological Perspectives on Dance.* New York: Congress on Research in Dance.

Rabiger, S. (1990) 'Art therapy as a container.' In C. Case and T. Dalley (eds) *Working with Children in Art Therapy.* London: Routledge.

Reason, P. (1994) 'Three approaches to participative inquiry.' In N.K. Denzin and Y.S. Lincoln (eds) *Handbook of Qualitative Research.* London: Sage.

Reiland, J.D. (1990) 'A preliminary study of dance/movement therapy with field-dependent alcoholic women.' *The Arts in Psychotherapy 17,* 4, 349–354.

Rennie, D.L. (1994) 'Storytelling in psychotherapy: the client's subjective experience.' *Psychotherapy 31,* 2, 234–243.

Ritter, M. and Low, K.G. (1996) 'Effects of dance/movement therapy: a meta-analysis.' *The Arts in Psychotherapy 23,* 3, 249–260.

Rogers, C. (1957) 'The necessary and sufficient conditions of therapeutic personality change.' *Journal of Consulting Psychology 21,* 2, 95–103.

Rogers, P. (1994) 'Sexual abuse and eating disorders: a possible connection indicated through music therapy?' In D. Dokter (ed) *Arts Therapies and Clients with Eating Disorders: Fragile Board.* London: Jessica Kingsley Publishers.

Rosal, M.L. (1993) 'Comparative group art therapy research to evaluate changes in locus of control in behaviour disordered children.' *The Arts in Psychotherapy 20,* 3, 231–242.

Russell, D.E.H. (1983) 'The incidence and prevalence of intrafamilial and extrafamilial sexual abuse of female children.' *Child Abuse and Neglect 7,* 133–146.

Russell, D.E.H. (1984) 'The prevalence of seriousness of incestuous abuse: stepfathers vs. biological fathers.' *Child Abuse and Neglect 8,* 15–22.

Sanderson, C. (1990, 1995) *Counselling Adult Survivors of Child Sexual Abuse,* 1st and 2nd edns. London: Jessica Kingsley Publishers.

Schmais, C. (1985) 'Healing processes in group dance therapy.' *American Journal of Dance Therapy 8,* 17–36.

Schmais, C. (1988) 'Creative arts therapies and shamanism: a comparison.' *The Arts in Psychotherapy 15,* 4, 281–284.

Sedney, M.A. and Brooks, B. (1984) 'Factors associated with a history of childhood sexual experience in a nonclinical female population.' *Journal of the American Academy of Child Psychiatry 23,* 2, 215–218.

Serrano, J. (1989) 'The arts in therapy with survivors of incest.' In H. Wadeson, J. Durkin and D. Perach (eds) *Advances in Art Therapy.* Chichester: Wiley.

Sheldon, H. (1988) 'Childhood sexual abuse in adult female psychotherapy referrals: incidence and implications for treatment.' *British Journal of Psychiatry 152,* 107–111.

Sheldrick, C. (1991) 'Adult sequelae of child sexual abuse.' *British Journal of Psychiatry 158* (suppl. 10), 55–62.

Shuttleworth, R. (1985) 'Metaphor in therapy.' *Journal of Dramatherapy 8*, 2, 8–18.

Simonds, S.L. (1992) 'Sexual abuse and body image: approaches and implications for treatment.' *The Arts in Psychotherapy 19*, 289–293.

Simonds, S.L. (1994) *Bridging the Silence: Non-verbal Modalities in the Treatment of Adult Survivors of Childhood Sexual Abuse.* London: Norton.

Sledge, W.H. (1977) 'The therapist's use of metaphor.' *International Journal of Psychoanalytic Psychotherapy 6*, 113–130.

Smith, D., Pearce, L., Pringle, M. and Caplan, R. (1995) 'Adults with a history of childhood sexual abuse: evaluation of a pilot therapy service.' *British Medical Journal 310*, 6 May, 1175–1178.

Spring, J. (1987) *Cry Hard and Swim.* London: Virago.

Stanton-Jones, K. (1992) *Dance Movement Therapy in Psychiatry.* London: Tavistock/Routledge.

Strauss, A. and Corbin, J. (1990) *Basics of Qualitative Research: Grounded Theory Procedures and Techniques.* London: Sage.

Strauss, A. and Corbin, J. (1994) 'Grounded theory methodology: an overview.' In N.K. Denzin and Y.S. Lincoln (eds) *Handbook of Qualitative Research.* London: Sage.

Suzuki, S. (1973) *Zen Mind, Beginner's Mind.* New York: Weatherhill.

Tardif, T.Z. and Sternberg, R.J. (1988) 'What do we know about creativity?' In R.J. Sternberg (ed) *The Nature of Creativity, Contemporary Psychological Perspectives.* Cambridge: Cambridge University Press.

Truax, C.B. and Carkhuff, R.R. (1967) *Toward Effective Counselling and Psychotherapy: Training and Practice.* Chicago: Aldine.

Tsai, M., Feldman-Summers, S. and Edgar, M. (1979) 'Childhood molestation: variables related to differential impacts on psychosexual functioning in adult women.' *Journal of Abnormal Psychology 88*, 4, 407–417.

Volkman, S. (1993) 'Music therapy in the treatment of trauma-induced dissociative disorders.' *The Arts in Psychotherapy 20*, 3, 243–251.

Walker, S. and James, H. (1992) 'Childhood physical and sexual abuse in women: report from a psychiatric emergency clinic.' *Psychiatry in Practice 11*, 1, 15–18.

Walker, E., Katon, W., Harrop-Griffiths, J., Holm, L., Russo, J. and Hickok, L.R. (1988) 'Relationship of chronic pelvic pain to psychiatric diagnoses and childhood sexual abuse.' *American Journal of Psychiatry 145*, 1, 75–80.

Walker, E.A., Katon, W.J., Roy-Byrne, P.P., Jemelka, R.P. and Russo, J. (1993) 'Histories of sexual victimization in patients with irritable bowel syndrome or inflammatory bowel disease.' *American Journal of Psychiatry 150*, 10, 1502–1506.

Waller, D. and Dalley, T. (1992) 'Art therapy: a theoretical perspective.' In D. Waller and A. Gilroy (eds) *Art Therapy: A Handbook.* Buckingham: Open University Press.

Waterhouse, R. and Strickland, S. (1994) 'Abuses of memory.' *Independent on Sunday,* 1 May 1994, 17.

Weissman, M.M. and Paykel, E.S. (1974) *The Depressed Woman.* Chicago: University of Chicago Press.

Wellman, M.M. (1993) 'Child sexual abuse and gender differences: attitudes and prevalence.' *Child Abuse and Neglect 17,* 539–547.

West, W. (1995) Integrating psychotherapy and healing: an inquiry into the experiences of counsellors and psychotherapists whose work includes healing. Unpublished PhD thesis, University of Keele.

Williams, L.M. (1994) 'Recall of childhood trauma: a prospective study of women's memories of child sexual abuse.' *Journal of Consulting and Clinical Psychology 62,* 6, 1167–1176.

Winnicott, D.W. (1965) 'The capacity to be alone.' In *The Maturational Processes and the Facilitating Environment.* London: Hogarth Press.

Winnicott, D.W. (1971) *Playing and Reality.* Harmondsworth: Penguin.

Yalom, I.D. (1975) *The Theory and Practice of Group Psychotherapy,* 2nd edn. New York: Basic Books.

Subject Index

Entries in italics refer to activities.

Author Index